T0147158

Launching
Vee's Chariot

An End-of-Life Tale

ALSO BY KATE RILEY

The Green Velvet Journals

Praise for *Launching Vee's Chariot*

"This is a conversation so real and engaging you feel like you are right there with this strong and articulate mother-daughter pair as they work together to find their way through to the end. And you will want to cheer them both on. Their story is a fearless exploration and an honest exposition of how nothing that has come before can quite prepare us for this time. Yet, when the time comes, there is nothing more important than being there and being present, no matter what. This is a book to read and keep: you will want your family to read it when your time comes, and you will want to read it while caring for one of them. It is a gift, a comfort, and a treasure."

~ **Bonnie Vestal, M.D.**, *Pediatric Oncologist and Medical Counselor, retired*

"Kate Riley's *Launching Vee's Chariot* sings with life as she shares her intimate journey of supporting her mother through her last days. Told with humor, honesty and compassion, her story is delightfully unique (wait until you meet her colorful, courageous, and spirited mother!). At the same time there is much here to resonate with and inspire us as we face the challenges, epiphanies, sorrows and joys that give such depth and richness to our living, grieving, and dying."

~ **Alexandra Kennedy**, *MA MFT,* Psychotherapist and author of *Honoring Grief, Losing a Parent,* and *The Infinite Thread: Healing Relationships Beyond Loss*

"Intuitive and insightful, Kate Riley is a natural storyteller, and she shares this mother-daughter journey from all angles as she witnesses, participates, and holds sacred space for her mother's death, a conscious dying process. This story is designed and told with whole-hearted courage, vulnerability and love ... and a dash of humor which brings moments of levity to perhaps one of the most painful gifts of a lifetime."

~ **Janet Lucy**, *MA MFT,* Award-winning author, *Moon Mother, Moon Daughter* and *The Three Sunflowers*

Balboa Press books may be ordered through booksellers or by contacting:

Balboa Press
A Division of Hay House
1663 Liberty Drive
Bloomington, IN 47403
www.balboapress.com
1 (877) 407-4847

Print information available on the last page.

ISBN: 978-1-5043-5652-7 (sc)
ISBN: 978-1-5043-5653-4 (e)

Library of Congress Control Number: 2016906566

Balboa Press rev. date: 05/10/2016

Launching Vee's Chariot

An End-of-Life Tale

KATE RILEY

BALBOA.
PRESS
A DIVISION OF HAY HOUSE

Note to the Reader

In order to preserve anonymity, most of the individual names and places as well as distinguishing details of individuals and settings have been changed. My intention throughout was to convey the truth and essence of everything I witnessed and experienced with the highest integrity. All events are true to the best of my knowledge. Some scenes have been deliberately compressed, especially near the end. It is the living tale of a dying woman told through narrative design. This work is solely intended for personal growth and education.

In loving memory of my parents, Vee & John Riley

VELMA "VEE" NADINE RILEY
September 11, 1927-September 7, 2014

The Path of Transformation

Life! Where are you taking me?
I'm stuck in a puddle of pain
seeking the unseen, I do my best
forging ahead with boundless courage.

I take action
reaching, reaching,
climbing, climbing
I raise the bar to a higher level.

Waking from the trance, I feel a shift.
There within is a palace of immense power
…my soul print.

Vee Riley

Contents

Foreword

There can be no question that the coming and going of one's life is a topic that affects us all. One day we arrive here from the ethers of the Divine One and--likewise--one day we shall return to It. Most of us are good with the coming part—it's the going part that we tend to avoid thinking about. This is a topic that deserves our attention because it is one that every one of us will have an opportunity to experience at some point; it is only a matter of when.

In her book, *Launching Vee's Chariot: An End-of-Life Tale*, Kate Riley exquisitely shares her own experience of this sacred sojourn with her mother, Vee. In this true story you will learn that dying a conscious death is perhaps one of the most empowering and beautiful events a human being can ever experience. Read this book and you'll discover a deeper reserve of inner peace than you have even known.

~ **Dr. Dennis Merritt Jones** Award winning author of, *The Art of Uncertainty - How to Live in the Mystery of Life and Love It,* and, *Your (Re)Defining Moments - Becoming Who You Were Born to Be*

Preface

In the beginning, my father was my champion. Then later, as you will find written among these pages, my mother became my champion. When both were gone from this world, I learned I was the champion of my own universe. This recognition culminated on completion of writing *Launching Vee's Chariot*. It was a total surprise, and along with it came great moral reckoning. People warned me about feeling abandoned, an orphan in a strange land. This was not at all the case.

I wrote this book because I had no other choice.

There are people, places, and events that happen in *Life*. How we choose to deal with our experiences is at the foundation for evolving and maturing into authentic beings. Vee made it to the finish line! While maintaining autonomy, she died on her own terms. This is the unabridged story. The story that begged to be told.

Landing at a crossroad, twenty-eight years ago, I trained with hospice in California. I had no other choice. I found the subject of death and dying intriguing (strange, given I so feared death as a youngster). Over time, I have had the opportunity, and pleasure, to sit with many at this incredibly profound juncture. A few were family members or acquaintances. Most were complete strangers. *All* taught me something about *Life* and *Death*. Albeit, no one shook me at the core like my mother!

For nine months, I was committed. After all, what does a daughter say to her mother after being asked, "Kate, will you lean into my dying?" Sitting on her bed that day, gazing into my mother's eyes, I captured everything Vee was made up of – a galaxy of stars, and light, and beauty. Expansion. There was no fear so I had no reason to generate my own. Love traveled on a golden thread between our hearts, and I knew without a doubt I would devote whatever time it took. I had no other choice. This required daily work on behalf of my own soul—hitting the psychological, physical, and emotional levels with a tough, almost feral abandon. A strong, uncompromising will took over. My psyche never let me off the hook. Part of the assignment entailed constant re-examination of my own thoughts, concerns, and fears. I traveled deep into the unknown and did so in a very different light than ever before. Whoever has lost someone very dear knows the challenges that arrive unannounced. There are no detailed road maps. Like many, I stumbled and fell into giant pools of despair and vulnerability, questioned family dynamics, and doubted my ability to continue.

All along, I was re-writing the narrative of my life. This was unconscious at the time. Then, when my mother died, I knew I had to sit down and write about one of the most profound events of my life. I spent hours mining my journals and those of my mother. Often my heart ached dangerously, and yet at times exploded with joy, during the nine months it took to write the original draft. I traveled beyond my ordinary range of attitudinal beliefs, absorbing, gestating and integrating the new mythologies. Ultimately, it was in the writing of *Launching* that I found acceptance, radical forgiveness, and peace of mind.

It is my hope that *Launching Vee's Chariot* finds a way into your heart and mind. And that somewhere each of you arrives at your own destination a bit changed. A bit braver. Compassionate and more loving. Maybe a bit more willing to accept *Death* as a part of *Life*. To imagine a wondrous place when our time here ends. To fully experience *Life*, we must accept *Death*; or at minimum accept the fact that we are all going to die one day. *Memento Mori!*

Kate Riley

Prologue

Before I step into this story, I offer below Vee's *Epilogue* from *The Green Velvet Journals*, a book we co-authored and published in 2004. Vee is as much a part of *Launching* as she was a part of *The Green Velvet Journals*. Her words reflect a clear testament to the true nature of a courageous woman who chose to follow her soul's path, always seeking to know her divine blueprint, regardless of circumstances.

"I began my soul's journey into wellness decades ago. Four and a half years ago [January 3, 2000], I discovered the mass in my breast and needed to reach even more deeply into my spiritual core to find healing. I felt a force directing me. A deep yearning to know and experience my truth formed the foundation of my search.

On this quiet Sunday afternoon, a feeling of tranquility floods my being. Sitting in the garden I share with the squirrels and blue jays, I take in the miracle of nature. The ivy-covered arbor covering the path to my doorway embraces the deer as well as friends, family, and clients. Beside the front door, the red Begonia tumbles out of its window box, an array of bold color more beautiful than ever. I marvel at the grand design of creation. Sipping my tea, I reflect upon my own divine blueprint for life.

We are born and we die – all of us. And between those points, we live our lives and grow our souls.

A favorite Chinese proverb reads, "Our destiny, or allotted time, is sealed; and when the door closes on life, it is by mandate of heaven." In my allotted time, I have journeyed far. Now, and until my door closes, I am blessed to live in joy and peace.

Today, here in my garden, I own a deeper understanding of the process that led me from one choice to another as I savor each precious moment of life.

Although my life continues to embrace a physical challenge, it is filled with a world of sacred places. I still dream dreams and have visions of beauty and wonder.

We always have choice. I have chosen to go within when faced with a decision, being the only one who can know the needs of my soul. Here is a verbal hug to my family and friends for allowing me to do this. The inner truth reveals only love.

I have chipped and pecked away at the shell of my limitation; in the shattering of the pieces, a new, more enlightened self broke free."

Vee Riley's Epilogue to *The Green Velvet Journals*
(In The Beam Publishing House 2004)

***

And below is Vee's last handwritten journal entry, dated August 27, 2014, shortly before her death:

Nick arrived yesterday. He is working on me hand and foot. Whatever that means. This afternoon he and Maryanne will do the healing session together. It will be a new beginning for us.

Nick will take my prayer and place it in the prayer wheel.

The universe already knows what I am thinking.

Let it go! Three single words but so very hard to do!

I must crack open the shell around me. Resistance to allowing myself to be free of this body and this world.

Today is all good with my decision.

PART I

The Opening

"As we consider how death makes life possible, we may become happier, healthier, and better citizens. Likewise, we may begin to renew our sense of purpose in the context of our rapidly changing times. We will lay the groundwork for a new way of understanding ourselves in the light of our own mortality and that of our loved ones."

Marilyn Schlitz, PhD
Author of *Death Makes Life Possible*

Chapter One

Silent Witness

"Mom, do you think you can get in the car?" I ask, feeling a mix of emotions.

"Oh, I don't know," Vee says, exhausted.

"Well, it's a trip we need to make. The roads are pretty clear right now. I promise to go slow, especially over the bumps and around the turn-about. You can just stay in your pajamas and robe. No one will care. Remember, we're in this together."

"Well, all right then." She is not the least bit happy about making the short trip. I'm not either but it's one *I* need to make.

My older sister Anna and I usher our mother out to my car. Noticing some residual snow still in the walkway, I hope to God she doesn't fall. Anna helps her climb in for what might be our mother's last car ride. There will be no seatbelt protection. Vee detests them since having breast and hip surgeries. I've never driven so slowly or carefully, not even when I had my newborn son in the car. Our mother winces in pain with every little bump in the road. I drive up under the porte cochere of St. Francis Hospital, where we wait in the warmth of the car until Anna retrieves a wheelchair. Silence fills the air. A light snow begins to fall. After our mother is safely transferred, I drive out to find a parking space but not before seeing her small head disappear through the automatic closing door.

Dr. Andrew Kastner called Vee last week and suggested she schedule an appointment so that he could go over the CT scans. All we knew at this point was the breast cancer she had fourteen years ago had metastasized. Having been a medical transcriber in radiology for twenty years, I knew this was not good news. Because Anna drove over at the last minute, Dr. Kastner agreed to see us at the end of his day. Once in the exam room, everything fell quiet, pensive, like waiting for a verdict no one wants.

Vee bows her head, yielding to what is coming, solemn in her usual contemplative way. Her left palm faces upward and rests in her other palm nestled in the folds of her pink terrycloth bathrobe. I wonder about her thoughts. The exam door opens and in walks Dr. Kastner, tall and thin, impeccably dressed, yet with bowtie slightly askew. I've never seen him wearing a white coat, which is why I trust him so much.

"Hello, Vee." He sets her chart down and takes a seat on the small round stool. He faces her with deliberate and full attention. Vee takes a moment to introduce her daughters. A quick nod of recognition lands on me and Anna and back to Vee. As he signs into the computer and begins to retrieve her recent CT scans, I study the images. Next, he methodically describes each CT slice where a tumor has been located. I sit up on the exam table as a silent witness. Anna sits nearby, one leg swinging back and forth over the other. Kastner is calm, but forthright in delivering the news. And then, with no notice, he pushes his stool back across the tiny room where he leans on the door. His delivery seems almost routine as he begins to inform Vee of her treatment options. He recommends a drug by the name of Zometa 4 mg IV, every three to four weeks, to reduce the probability of further pathologic fractures and lets her know that, because she is otherwise healthy, she may well live long enough to see the bone metastases manifest considerable suffering. And then, without taking a breath, he recommends she consult with Dr. Derek Bradshaw regarding the possibility of palliative radiation. *What? Wait a minute! This would mean driving out of town.* Does Dr. Kastner actually think that because Vee had a positive experience with radiation therapy twelve years ago, she is going to go for it now? At 87! Studying my mother, I know precisely her thoughts. Going to Summerville, over an hour's drive one-way, three times a week, is not an option. She holds steady and doesn't blink an eye. Something is coming.

"I thought you were going to be *with me* until the very end," she says spellbound. This is one of the saddest moments of my life.

"And I am *with you*." He is genuinely respectful of her honest disclosure. Kastner went on to explain that he was giving her some options for treatment. I vaguely recall Vee letting him know back in January that she would not be pursuing medical intervention and that she was comfortable with her mortality. After a brief pause, I ask, "So, what's the worst possible scenario here?" For some dumb reason, I feel I need to know. What does the warning label say about nine malignant tumors? What is the expiration date? I never once hear what I need to hear, a real end-of-life dialogue. If Kastner did speak of this, it rolled right over me.

We leave the exam room and travel as a small unit down the hallway. There is nothing like being in a clinic after hours. Anna pushes the wheelchair up to the double doors where I exit to retrieve my car. As soon as our mom is in the front seat again, we wait in silence until Anna returns from dropping off the wheelchair. I feel as though I'm seated in an airtight compression chamber somewhere suspended in the middle of space, not moving, waiting. Anna gets in the backseat and breaks my spell. I fall back into real time when she shuts the car door.

"Now why would I do that?!" Vee exclaims.

The more she thinks about the visit, the angrier she becomes.

"Mom!" I say, "As your physician, Dr. Kastner had to give you some treatment options. It's part of his job. It doesn't mean that you have to do those things or that he even supports treatment. He can't just deliver news like that without giving you some options to think about. Besides, it's still your choice, all the way!"

"And I don't even know why you had to ask that question, Kate!"

I don't respond.

We drive the short distance back to Vee's Place in silence. Pulling into her driveway, I sigh a huge relief. At least she is still living at home. Her plan, since moving to this incredible valley more than a decade ago, has been to remain below Pyramid Mountain until her life is over. Walking her back inside, I silently make the commitment to do everything in my power to support my mother's final wishes.

Chapter Two

Conscious Dying

Our roles as mother and daughter were rapidly changing, although I was oblivious to it at the time. I'm reasonably sure Vee felt the same way. People tend to move about in their predicted roles even after news such as this. Vee knew she was going to die without treatment and I knew I would stay with her until the very end. What that picture looked like, or her allotted time, was as mysterious as death itself.

We both came away from Dr. Kastner's office needing time to integrate the news. Anna immediately returned to her home three hours away. I allowed Vee the time she needed and decided I would wait for her to make the first move. I remember asking her before the office visit whether Dr. Kastner had called her with the CT scan results. She had responded, "No, it doesn't really matter. It won't change anything." She went to his office that day, I believe, for the benefit of her children. She had already made up her mind to die a conscious death. All I could do now was hold space for her, making every single remaining moment sacred. That was my vow.

* * *

"Kate, I had a really bad night last night. The pain kept me awake." She sounds weary.

"I'll be over after I walk Bailey."

"Okay. Thanks."

Holland, my partner of ten years, visits only on the weekends. I explain to him that I will most likely be at Vee's Place for the day, and he volunteers to take Bailey, our yellow lab, for a long hike. I'm immediately relieved as the guilt of having to leave Bailey alone more and more is beginning to surface.

Arriving, I find my mother standing before her dining room table. Papers are strewn across a bright spring yellow tablecloth, small Easter chocolates wrapped in glistening pastels pushed aside. She is bundled up in a baby-blue terrycloth robe. One whole side looks as though she's used it as an apron. I have to smile at the mustard yellow handprints. She turns and looks at me with an expression that holds fear and uncertainty, a rarity in Vee.

"I need to sell my car to pay for my cremation. I can't find the title."

We search through piles of papers. When I locate my parents' marriage certificate, I study it carefully. After inspecting every document without locating the Subaru title we move into the living room and sit in front of the fire. My mother is depleted of all energy.

"I just want everyone to let me die. I've had a full life and I have no regrets. My soul is calling me back."

I stare at her intently, in hopes of gaining more knowledge, a clue, a detailed map with explicit routes including a timeline. *Anything.* Near the end of a long silence, I detect a slight shift.

"I think it's going to happen really fast," she adds with enthusiasm.

I can't help wondering whether she said this out of a deep desire for her own good or mine. What's *fast* in soul time? The soul doesn't operate in time and space. My intuition is telling me it's all okay. Everything is happening according to divine order, something Vee believed and passed my way during all of my adult life. Besides, searching for answers hidden in the mystery gets us nowhere. Together we bask in the warmth of the fire. Despite her pain and fatigue, she is radiating peace and exquisite beauty, her eyes knowing and soulful. For now, this is enough to carry me along in the mystery.

"Everything seems so surreal," she says smiling.

"You know, I stood in front of my fireplace this morning and said to Holland, 'I feel like I've entered into another realm. Everything seems so surreal.'"

"I know it!" she says with excitement. And it was exciting, on some level, I have to admit.

For most of the day, Vee continued to organize and plan for whatever time she had left. And while we hadn't located the car title, another shift had clearly taken place. I watched as my mother carefully took inventory of what needed to be done. It mostly involved her one and only bank account, a small petty cash supply, and calling a few friends to say goodbye. Suddenly she taps her forehead like she does whenever an insight comes to her. She pauses for a moment and then takes a seat at the dining room table, adjusting the large yellow pillow that supports her back. She reaches in the stack of blank notecards and immediately begins writing a note. After sealing the envelope, she hands it to me. "Here take this to the post office when you go to the grocery store. Oh, and I need coffee."

Immediately, I sense an urgent letter of atonement given the name on the envelope. She isn't leaving one stone unturned. Upon my return from town, she has already made arrangements for someone to come in and repair the drywall in her master bath. Everything needs to be in order and it is important that nothing be left for her three children to have to deal with. She has already joined FCAI

(Funeral Consumer's Alliance of Idaho) to ensure a locked in price for cremation. I mention that Holland is thinking about purchasing her Subaru for his daughter. My mother is relieved because now she will have the cash to pay for her cremation. Last year, she and I met with Dr. Kastner to discuss the POST (Physician's Order of Scope of Treatment) which he had signed. After locating it, we tape it to the wall next to her bed. More recently she met Susan Randall with whom she developed an immediate rapport. Susan is my partner in death and dying work. We both trained under Jerrigrace Lyons of Final Passages and the plan was that we would be handling Vee's death care. My mother makes it clear she doesn't want a home funeral with a lot of visitors stopping by, only a few.

After a long day of taking care of business matters, Vee calls her sister and brother and then Sara. Within an hour after hanging up, I learn that Sara has booked a plane ticket and is scheduled to arrive Tuesday night. I feel enormous relief that my younger sister is coming.

The next day, I order a hospital bed. Part of helping my mother die a peaceful death is to help create a peaceful setting. When the bed is delivered, I am speechless and left standing in shock. The bed is old and decrepit, chocolate brown with cold hard metal handrails. Thinking about how many people have died in this bed, I pull out a sage stick and go to work. After covering most of the metal with pink blankets and pillows I drive into town to purchase pink roses, lots of them. Within an hour, Vee's new suite reflects an aesthetic beauty even though it masks impending death. When I reposition the bed, Vee has an unobstructed view of her backyard. The reconfiguration makes a huge difference in the way the light streams through. Soon she will watch tree limbs and leaves dance against the blinds as the sun sets behind Bellow Mountain. This would later become a nightly ritual. Since we were beginning to change the language around certain things, we decide on naming the bed *The Royal Roost*. Vee settles comfortably in between the pink flannel sheets as if she is ready to die now. I'm wondering whether she might die that very night.

"Thank you, Kate, for everything. You've done a lot!"

After cleaning up the dinner dishes, I return and sit bedside with her. She opens her eyes and I know immediately she has something important to say.

"Kate, I can't open the dryer door anymore. And I can barely open the refrigerator. I have to use both hands now."

The pain is getting worse. I can tell by the way she winces and cries out at times, even when she barely moves. She is adamantly against pain meds, particularly morphine. I rise and cross the room to close her blinds.

"Kate, will I remain conscious if I eat marijuana cookies? Someone told me they would help with the pain."

"You could always try some."

Arriving the next morning, I find my mother at the kitchen table.

"Well, I'm still here!" Sensing her frustration, I can't help thinking how much the ego is involved and how we, as humans, need to let go of the ego in order to die. Suddenly, I have the idea to interview and film my mom on the subject of *conscious dying.* In one interview she said:

> "We talk about conscious dying, but it's not easy. I've experienced this. I thought that when I made up my mind to go, I would just go! It's not that easy. I need to complete some more things, probably some that I am unaware of, that spirit is asking me to do, to complete, before I die. And when I have completed that, then I believe I will go."

During several filming episodes, I sense her becoming more thoughtful on the subject—mindfully choosing her words. My mother is clearly taking responsibility for everything involving her life and her death. More than anything, my wish is for her to orchestrate a *good*, conscious death. However, in recent days, I notice my mother has become somewhat incapacitated and daily tasks are becoming increasingly difficult, if not impossible. She has growing and legitimate concern about how long this is actually going to take, and about the physical toll on her body. That answer is precisely what I wanted from Dr. Kastner. But this is Vee's death, not the death I might want for her. I must remain grounded in the knowing that everything is in perfect order. With that, I need to remain in the present, mindful to take good care of my mother, and to appreciate this very short time together.

If Vee had died that night, my view on conscious dying would have remained the same. I actually believed that because of her intent and willingness to let go, it would happen very soon. In fact, I had a secret wish that it would all happen in a very simple manner, that she would be right about it all. I had even pictured Vee crawling in between her flannel sheets, wearing her favorite pink pajamas, maybe downing a shot of vodka, and speaking her final words, "Goodnight Moon! It's all perfect!" But it didn't happen this way. Apparently, she still had work to do.

Chapter Three

Exit Plans

Sara arrives and we make plans to drive together to Summerville to pick up a cardboard cremation container. I am so relieved she is going with me. Honestly, I'm not sure I could do it alone. We pack a picnic and decide to head to the lake and visit familiar places from our childhood. Traveling along Lakeview Drive, I suggest driving by our old house. Sara, in her usual amenable state, agrees. It is surprising how a long street from your childhood becomes shorter over time. And the house! I remember a one-level brick ranch house, with extended hallways that wound around to all the bedrooms. Even before I pull up to the circular driveway, I remember everything. It was June 8, 1968. I was thirteen years old. Dad was at work and Mom was pulling out of the garage. I was babysitting. Suddenly, *something* told me to check the baby's room. There in the center of the crib, I found the baby, blue and not breathing. After resuscitation and hospitalization, the baby lived. She now sits next to me in the cab of the borrowed truck.

"I don't remember any of it," Sara says, staring at the ranch house.

Given the circumstances, she and I enjoy our picnic. We share a Corona and talk about memories. After taking some pictures, we head to the funeral home. The director is expecting us. It's not easy picking up a cremation container for your mother's body. We move through the necessary actions, both staring at the retort. I notice the buttons that will be pushed to ignite the burners. After loading the cardboard box into the bed of the truck, Sara and I stop at a nursery on the way out of town. I remember my mom saying, "If you love me, plant a tree." We pick out a Siberian pine and a rose bush called, "Always and Forever." Tears flow while we situate the tree inside the partially assembled cremation container. Sara carries the white satin pillow to the cab of the truck as if it's a newborn baby.

Parking in the driveway at Vee's Place, I unload the Siberian pine and set it near the walkway. I will have Holland plant it next weekend. Sara and I carefully unload the cremation box and place it in the garage. Neither of us is in the mood for assembling the long box lined with white satin. Sara carries the white satin pillow inside. We find our mother in her living room.

"Passover would be a great day to leave. I thought about Easter too!"

I can't help smiling. I'm getting used to conversing about her exit plans. Sara, however, is not. I sense a moment of discomfort as she sets the white pillow down on a chair.

Before I leave to return home, Vee smiles and reiterates, "I've had a full life." She had clearly been working on acceptance while we were away. On my way home, I wondered whether she wanted to die while Sara was visiting.

Anna's plan is to drive over the following day so the Riley girls, and their mother, will all be together. I pray and pray for harmony. I even add us to prayer lists all over the map and ask my sisterhood to pray. Maybe the daughters will help their mother collage her cremation container, maybe not. We didn't. The time came for Anna to take Sara to the airport, and after pensive goodbyes, my sisters leave Vee's Place. I wonder if my sisters will see our mom again. A few minutes later, I find my mom in the laundry room peering out into the garage. The cardboard container is now propped up on the spare massage table, assembled and ready.

"Oh it looks just like a baby buggy!" She giggles with delight. Before turning off the lights, she takes one more peek.

***

It's April 22nd when Vee decides to begin the collage work. I bring in about twenty magazines from her garage. She sits at the dining room table tearing out pictures and words. She prefers the rough edges in her collage work and wouldn't think of using scissors.

"Mom, I'm feeling like I need to go home and work on my presentation for the wellness festival."

"Go! I don't need anyone here when I die!" She is adamant. However, there is an underlying tone of edginess. It must be awful waiting to die when you have nine malignant lesions growing in various places within your torso. It's getting harder for her to breathe. Coughing and sneezing are out of the picture, even laughter, but sometimes she can't help herself.

Later, I return to Vee's Place. She is already in bed, tired and weak. We discuss what might be of help to her and come up with the plan to drum. My mom taught me the "heartbeat" beat at least a decade ago. The idea now is to drum and take it to a very slow "heartbeat," both of us visualizing her heart matching the beat of the drum. I take the drum Vee made years ago into my hands. As I prepare, my mother closes her eyes and crosses her thin hands over her chest. I drum, my gaze steady on her chest. After a while, I begin to slow the beat and eventually cease all drumming. In the silence, I find complete acceptance. Such reverence for my mother.

The next day, Vee and I learn that meals will be delivered twice a week, which is a tremendous relief. We consider moving the cremation container back out to the garage. People will be dropping in more often now. The lid to the cremation container is laid out across the dining room table. We joke about where we will dine.

"Let's get some champagne and launch this thing!" She giggles and then flinches in pain. She has handwritten *Vee's Chariot* on a thin piece of bark and has already attached it to the end of the lid. A large silver glittery star rests on top. She points at it and says with a twinkle in her eye, "I am the star of my own show." In the midst of preparing and planning, Vee still has her sense of humor.

"Call Alex and ask her to come over for the launch party!" Alex has been a good friend of Vee's and I am so grateful for everything she is doing. She is the one responsible for scheduling meal drop-offs. I don't know how I will even begin to thank her, but I can't think about that now.

"Quick, let's pick out something from my house that she might like." Together our eyes fall on the copper kaleidoscope my mom purchased in Cambria, California. Vee has me wrap it in tissue paper and place it in a gift box. Lately, she has been giving things away. She even held an art show recently, stating, "Everything in the house is for sale. Everything!"

Alex arrives with piping hot french fries from a favorite local restaurant. After we pour the Prosecco, Alex opens her gift. Vee and I both knew she would love it.

"Alex, would you mind helping me carry this lid back out to the garage?"

"No, not at all." She is amazed at all the progress we've made. It's nearly finished, and I'm wondering whether my mother is waiting for the completion of the Chariot. It does seem more fitting to complete the artwork before she dies, especially since she is the one taking responsibility to finalize her affairs.

While in the garage, I get this silly idea to place the cremation container up on the luggage rack of Vee's Subaru. Then I get behind the wheel and ask Alex to take my picture driving. The rest of the evening we spend sipping Prosecco with Vee. It is lovely, and I leave for my place hoping *the launch*, for Vee's sake, will be sooner rather than later.

The next morning while having my coffee, I write a love letter to my mom. While reading it over, my heart begins to break wide open. My plan is to glue the letter to the foot of *Vee's Chariot*. Somehow I think it will help me when I am pushing my mother's body into the retort for cremation.

> *Dear Mom,*
>
> *Thank you for everything you have been to me.*
> *Thank you for raising me to always listen to my heart, to follow my passion.*
> *Thank you for teaching me to trust my voice, and to use my voice.*
> *Thank you for accepting me as I am, always.*
> *Thank you for showing me what happens when you follow your intuition.*
> *Thank you for allowing me to care for you at the end of your life.*
> *And finally...thank you for loving me.*
> *Dance your way into the next dimension with one great big exhalation!*

***

Packing my car for a quick trip, I'm relieved several friends and hospice will be coming around to help Vee. There are a few out-of-town clients I simply can't put off any longer. When I arrive at Vee's Place, I notice her bedroom door is closed. After a light knock, I open the door. My mother is in bed, her eyes closed. Maryanne, a friend of hers who does energy work, is there. Her hands are under Vee's feet but she nods for me to enter. My mom throws me a distant glance, starts to pull her hand out from under the cover but changes her mind. She has already let me go. I sob all the way to her driveway and down the highway before calling Judith, a very dear friend of Vee's. I had a two-hour drive ahead of me and knew Judith would say the perfect thing.

"We're all actors playing out our roles. You and your mother have said goodbye before, in other lifetimes. She is doing it right this time. It's *her* way. Know the truth and that you are a part of doing it right and doing it well."

Upon my return a few days later, I ask my mom to write her own obituary. She does so thinking it will be the last thing she ever writes. She reads it over quietly, and then, again methodically—line by line. After crossing out the last paragraph, she hands it to me for typing. She speaks softly, "I just want everyone to let me die."

"And I believe you have the support of your whole family, Mom."

"I am dying consciously. I had no way of knowing it would be happening this way or when. I don't know when. It's like having a baby. The baby comes when the baby comes. For now, I will continue to practice the art of dying. Dying can be very blissful because it puts you in a place of unconditional love."

Sean, my son, visits from Boise. He is getting ready for a big trip to walk the Camino de Santiago in Spain. He sits outside, next to Grammy, on the Riley bench. I remain inside Vee's Place. After spending the afternoon together talking, Sean gets ready to leave. I head back outside just as he tells her to look for him on the Camino after she dies. As he leaves to cross the yard, he and Grammy continue with tradition. "I love you more than you love me." Sean shouts back, "No, Grammy, I love you more than you love me!" They are both smiling and waving childlike to each other.

***

We're coming up on the end of May. It has been five months since our visit with Dr. Kastner. I have a presentation and workshop planned at this year's Sun Valley Wellness Festival. The closer we get, the more vulnerable I'm feeling, not because of my presentation, but because my mom could die right before the presentation. Moreover, it's getting harder to see my mom in pain. I wonder whether her rib cage is beginning to collapse. I've learned that micro-fractures can occur with rib lesions. On occasion, she shouts out in pain, and because of this bouts of unexpected grief start to hit me hard. I am blindsided tonight while eating a Caesar salad. Yesterday, I was overtaken while standing at the meat counter at the grocery store. Grief is random, and I continue to seek strength in my vulnerability. Sometimes I find it there.

I ask both my sisters to mail me a strand of their hair. I have an idea to weave these strands through our mother's hands after dressing her in the white silk robe she has selected to wear upon her death. They comply, but I'm starting to feel an undercurrent of unspoken resentment. We sisters are beginning to disband, which is, sadly, a common occurrence at the time of a death. I'm becoming a part of another matrix, existing in another place, another world, a world where I am no longer a part of the same tribe. We three girls were a strong team when our father was in the ICU, but that was seven years ago and much has happened in the intervening years. I recognize, now, the need to cultivate acceptance of our differences, and by accepting the change—monumental as it feels at times—I am then free to fully lean into my mother's dying process. Once again, I rely on the wisdom of my soul to carry me through.

"Kate, I believe that I contracted with all the people in my life. That's why I had trouble with them! It's all okay now."

I was sitting bedside when Vee spoke these words. She had many close friends and acquaintances. I knew she had forgiven the ones she needed to forgive. So many people die holding grudges, and I can't imagine what this does in the end. It must play a role. For now, I watch her look at the ceiling, her hands crossed over her shrinking chest cavity.

"Maybe I'll die in my bed or maybe I'll die on my massage table. I've done everything I need to do. Kate, if you need to clear something in our relationship, then that is something you need to do. As far as I'm concerned, I've done all my work."

Chapter Four

Rising Stardom

"Hi, Mom."

"Oh, hi."

"How are you?"

"I'm fine. After a pause, she queries, "I thought you were at Diana Nyad's reception?"

"I am. I've just met a producer who happens to be filming a documentary on death and dying."

"Oh, that's nice."

"Well, he's asked me if he can film you."

"When is he thinking about doing this?"

"Um, right now."

"Right now? Oh gosh."

"Yeah. I know it's short notice, really short notice, but he's flying out tomorrow at noon and won't be coming back to Sun Valley. He is actually here showing the premiere of his documentary, *The Embrace of Aging*. It's the one I attended yesterday afternoon."

"Well, I guess so. Are you guys coming here?"

"Yes. Keith, that's his name, Keith Famie. He's looking for a cameraman right now. Holland and I will have him follow us to your place."

"Well, okay."

We arrive at Vee's Place, and I approach the front door with trepidation. Anna has arrived today and is planning on spending two nights. I'm relieved but concerned about how she will take the filming. We walk in and immediately I sense Anna's unease. After a brief introduction, Keith goes to work. He is particularly taken by *Vee's Chariot*, which we bring into the living room. Anna stays in the guest room despite Keith's invitation to film her with Vee. He is gracious and respects everyone's place. The first film segment is taken outside, but we're rushed because the sunlight is fading. One of the film segments is of me walking Vee down the path from her meditation garden. I so want Anna on the other side of our mom. We then move inside where Keith has Vee place her bare feet on the lid of the Chariot. He asks her questions about her dying. As she begins to speak, I notice Holland standing nearby with his hand over his mouth, watching, speechless. I believe this is the first time he has been in the company of someone so intimately involved in a conversation about their own death. My mother doesn't surprise me anymore.

Keith asks whether he can return the next morning to finish filming. We've run out of natural light inside as well. He indicates the need for more footage. He'd like to film Vee again, and me, individually. He is respectful of my morning presentation at the Sun Valley Wellness Festival, so we agree to meet at 7 a.m. My mom jokes about hoping to have had her shower by then. When I hug her, I whisper, "Mom, thank you so much. This is really going to help people."

"Well, I guess I *am* the star of my own show," she replies with humility.

The following morning, we catch Vee walking from the kitchen with a cup of hot coffee and wearing her blue bathrobe. The mustard yellow handprints are gone. She has bed hair but is only slightly embarrassed and says, "You guys! I haven't even had my coffee yet!" Suddenly she doesn't look like a woman who is dying. Keith tells her to take her time while he sets up. I'm jittery. Anna is somewhere in the house, out of view, and I'm presenting in two hours. I meet Anna coming out of the bathroom and apologize. In that moment, I feel nothing but compassion for her. I even have compassion for her miniature dachshund, who is visibly shaking. Even his routine has been shaken up. I turn and head into the living room knowing there is nothing more I can say.

Keith knows precisely what he wants and is conscientious and smooth in directing everyone. He has managed to find a local professional cameraman, who arrives and begins setting up. Vee exits her bedroom not having showered and still looking great, considering her condition. She is wearing maroon velvet pants and a white fluffy waist length house-jacket and a brightly colored scarf. She is careful taking the two steps down into her sunken living room and then takes a seat near her Chariot. My mother is clearly giving it her all right now. Ben starts filming while Keith asks me a few questions. His last inquiry does me in. "Kate, if you could say one last thing to your mother, what would it be?" I glance in the direction of my mom. She sits slumped forward, eager to hear what I have to say. The twinkle in her eyes is still present. The heartache I'm feeling is unbearable.

"I am really going to miss you, Mom." It's all I can muster.

Keith and Ben film one more segment with just me. Leaving Vee's Place, I turn into a complete mess.

Susan and I head out to the Sun Valley Inn. I've managed to trigger a memory in Susan of her own mother's death. Now both of us are crying. The flood gates have opened! I'm nearly hysterical, seriously contemplating whether or not I'm going to be able to present. On the way, we stop at the local mortuary to pick up a cardboard cremation container. We plan to use it in the workshop that follows our presentation. Entering the dark gloomy building, we search for the director. Thankfully, we've stopped sobbing. We chat for a few moments with the director and an employee before leaving. As Susan and I carry the six-foot long assembled container out of the mortuary, I notice several drivers staring at us. *Did they think we had someone inside?* The thought alone unmasks a devious smile. Fortunately, by the time we arrive in Sun Valley, we have pulled ourselves together. When we enter, we are surprised to find the room filling with people. Susan and I were concerned no one would choose to attend a presentation titled: *Death and Dying: Shifting the Paradigm*, especially at 9:00 a.m. on a Saturday morning. I ditch my previously planned presentation and decide to come from the place of vulnerability. Vee would have said, "Just shoot straight from the heart, Kate!"

Death makes us raw. Death makes us vulnerable. Vee had moved out of her vulnerable state and passed us all up. She was confident in her decision to die. She was the star of her own show, and I was the apprentice. She *knew* something six months ago when Susan and I were working on our presentation proposal. I remember Vee smiling and saying, "Well, it looks like I might be helping you guys after all."

Returning to Vee's Place, elated that the presentation went very well, I find Anna packing. She is leaving earlier than scheduled and will not be spending another night. I share chocolate covered strawberries that I picked up at Kontitorei Restaurant in Sun Valley, a gesture of peace. As she pulls out of the driveway, I feel helpless. Vee tells me not to worry. She adds, "*It's all perfect!*" But in my world, it's not.

Chapter Five

Insights on the Edge

Arriving at Triple Peak Ranch, about an hour from Pinedale, Wyoming, I enter my room at the end of the hall. All the rooms have personalized names. Mine is the Butch Cassidy Room. I'm facilitating two writing retreats, back to back, and already I feel a burden lifting from my shoulders. I'm here because I want to be. I need a break from Vee, and, moreover, she probably needs one from me. Her longtime friend Siouxze is staying with her.

During our first day, someone yells, "Moose!" We all jump up and run to the back door to watch a mama moose with her calf. The owners tell me they've named the baby *Kate*, after the Duchess of Cambridge. Suddenly, Mama jumps a barbed wired fence. She keeps walking while Kate runs frantically back and forth. I sense the panic and wonder whether Mama will go back and help her baby, who is obviously distraught. I can't help thinking about what animal might be lurking in the willows. We wait and watch. Finally, Kate jumps and clears the fence. Mama is teaching the little one. And I think about all that my own mother is teaching me in her death. What a vulnerable place for both Kates, each of us taking a leap into the unknown.

Later that evening, I head up to sleep with Butch. Grabbing my Ted Andrews *Animal-Speak* book, I open to Moose. Andrews writes:

> Keynote: Primal Feminine Energies and Magic of Life and Death. The moose can teach the ability to move from the outer world to the inner. It can teach how to cross from life to death and back to stronger life. It teaches how to use the thin thread that separates life and death to one's advantage. You cannot discuss the power of the moose without also discussing its antlers. Their antlers are the largest of all antlered animals. Antlers are ancient symbols of antenna—of crownings that activate the upper chakras of the head. When moose comes into your life, the primal contact with the great feminine force and void of life is being awakened. It is an invitation to learn to explore new depths of awareness and sensitivity within yourself and within your environs.

I think about all that Vee has taught me about the chakras. Crawling into bed, I whisper a prayer, "Kate, align yourself with this unique and sacred energy. It has been there all along in your relationship with Vee. Keep it, hold it, honor it, bless it, and thank it all, daily and forever." I drift off with fresh insight into my changing relationship with Anna and Sara and sense that I am entering into a new level of acceptance.

The next day, one of the writers tells me if I need to get right back to my mother, he is happy to drive me. I am completely taken aback by his offer and want to cry. He's aware I drove here alone and is sensitive enough to know if I get a call, I may be too vulnerable to drive the six hours' home. Later I think about how brave an offer it really is. Rob doesn't know what he might have in the seat next to him—a hysterical woman crying all the way or worse, having to endure the primal wail. I've found myself in both states more than once.

I'm blessed with one more sighting of Kate and her mama before the first retreat ends. It feels good to be a part of the lives of serious writers all working towards finished manuscripts. I have a few days before the next intensive. After my farewells to everyone, I settle in upstairs and call Vee.

"I'm trying to figure out what I'm supposed to do with the rest of my life. I don't understand it, Kate. It's all happening, so I'll just let it happen. It will all happen the way it will happen. I'm here and I'm happy."

"Do you want me to return? I just ended the first intensive."

"No!"

"What about Anna?"

"Kate, there is vulnerability around death, and Anna is angry and anxious about my death."

I'm struck by my mother's comment and question whether it holds true but then choose not to place more energy into it. It's not mine to hold or even begin to figure out.

We agree to talk the next day. I light a candle in my guest room and pray for Anna and Sara. I begin to wonder whether Anna thinks the whole movie filming was about fulfilling some grandiose wish for myself. After all, I was always doing something while we were younger to *outperform* her. I sit with my thoughts, staring at the flame of the small cobalt blue candle. *Kate! That was then. They don't know who you are now.* Rising to blow out the candle, I prepare for bed. Drifting off, I dream about Vee. Upon waking, I write details of the dream in my journal:

> My mom dies and I awaken just after the dream.
> The details are sketchy and I try to recall the dream.
> What I do know is there are three parts. Someone

tells me my mom is going to die. She dies. And then I'm with her (I think).

The following day, I call to check in. My mom sounds good. "Maryanne came over earlier and gave me another treatment. I saw all these colors and then I thought I stopped breathing. She did too and she even checked my pulse."

Hanging up, I'm torn with staying at Triple Peak for the second group of writers arriving in two days. My writer friend Angela is flying in from New York. I hate to cancel. I'm excited and have the energy to facilitate a new group. My friend Laurel and I talk about options. But as the sun begins to set, we decide to hit the road. She has offered to drive me and tells me we can figure out how to get my car back home later. I make the necessary call to the next group of writers. They understand.

Arriving at Vee's Place the following morning, I find her on the massage table practicing the art of dying. I've been away less than a week and can't help noticing more signs of her shrinking away. An already petite woman, my mother is now disappearing before my eyes.

"I've been meditating. I keep moving towards God's eye again. Kate, it's clearly an eye, God's eye. It's oval." Closing her eyes as if she might miss something, I leave her room. She must have forgotten about our phone conversation while I was deciding whether or not to return home early. Clearly, she's doing what she needs to do.

Vee comes and goes, in and out, all day. Settling into *The Royal Roost* for the night, she tells me she's glad I'm back. We say goodnight, and Laurel gives me a massage on Vee's table in the studio. I feel loved and taken care of in the full moon rising. Closing my eyes, I think I see the eye of God.

Chapter Six

The Lioness Roars

While sitting across from Vee at her dining room table, I notice she is exhausted. So am I. *How long is this going to go on?* Her breakfast is lighter than usual. She's been such a hearty eater all her life, so I wonder whether her body is beginning to shut down. The color in her eyes is changing ever so slightly, the white not as white. She seems void of spirit.

"I need you to sweep the hardwood floors again. And there are clothes in the washer that need to go into the dryer. I thought hospice was coming today, but they can't. So the dishes from yesterday are piling up. My sheets are due for a change." My mother has gathered as much steam as possible to deliver these words. It's becoming more and more difficult for both of us. She clearly wants to exit this world. And I am beginning to question my role as primary caregiver. *Can I continue?*

"I also need you to go by the post office and mail something when you go into town. It's important it goes out in today's mail."

After a delayed pause, she hands me a small white envelope, and I notice it's addressed to Sara. My intuition tells me it's her rent money. Sara has been struggling to make ends meet. I have given up work and income for the last seven months in order to be available for Vee. I'm using Holland's Discover card for our food. None of this feels right.

"You know what, Mom?! There is something seriously wrong! I have been helping you every single day. I've given up my work to be here for you! I'm not getting paid one single dime, and yet you continue to help cover Sara's rent! Jesus!!!"

Vee sits across from me, staring in silence. When I finish, I feel terrible. *God, why are my sisters not helping? I don't understand.* My mom and I rise from the dining room table. She heads into her bedroom and closes her door. I go and change the laundry and then open the door to the garage to grab the broom and dustpan. Pausing, I find myself staring at the Chariot and completely cave.

After my chores are completed, I retrieve the small white envelope from the dining room table. I don't even check on my mom before leaving the house. I'm in no place for an apology yet. I walk uneasily to my car. *God, I need to get grounded.* Pulling out for the post office, my eyes scan her property. *Come back and work the land, Kate!*

Upon my return, I check in on Vee and then head up the stone pathway to the meditation garden on the hillside. As I begin weeding, I meditate on clearing a staircase to heaven and focus deliberately on weeding negative thoughts and fears from my mind. I try to find the sacredness in small things like the tiny dandelions creeping up from under heavy stones. And then, suddenly, I recall the dreadful scene that recently took place at my condo before Sean left for Spain. *How could I have possibly left a two-gallon water jug on the kitchen counter without telling my own son it was filled with bleach?* As I inch my way up the stone walkway, I think about how sick he was that night after gulping down a glass. I force corrosive thoughts of him dying out of my mind. Out of the blue, two ravens swoop down over my head and back up to land on my mother's roof. After weeding the pathway, I sit for a long time in the meditation garden. It was nearly a decade ago that we began creating this sacred outdoor garden. Over time, the whole family added special plants and trees, rocks and birdbaths. Every tree is named after one of us. It warms me to know that Vee is dying on the property she so cherished.

Getting my mom settled in for the night, I leave and think about my role in the family dynamics. Maybe I need to back off so that my sisters can be more involved. Heading home, I plan to email them an invitation.

That night I dream about a lioness. The next morning, I wake and write about it:

> I'm walking down a pathway that is about to make a
> hair-pin turn to the right. There are trees and rocks
> and the terrain is rough. Before I get to the bottom
> to make another decision on which way to go, I stop
> where another road intersects the one I'm traveling.
> Looking where that road leads, I notice a very large
> lioness making her way over some rocks. She appears
> to be heading in our direction. I tell the man I'm
> with about it. (Holland?) He is not concerned. Up
> the road, I see a building and run in where I find
> there is only one room. Looking across the room I
> notice a large opening in the wall (where a window
> might be but without glass). Crouching down below
> the opening, I sense the lioness is right outside
> and very close. In fear I sit peering up towards the
> opening, expecting her to jump up and through the
> window, but she never does. I wake up.

Retrieving my bible, *Animals-Speak*, by Ted Andrews I look up
Lion:

> Keynote: Assertion of the Feminine and the Power
> of the Female Sun. If a lion has shown up as a totem,
> you can expect lessons and issues dealing with
> community and groups to surface. There may be a
> need to examine your own role in the group. When
> a lion has shown up, there will be opportunity to
> awaken to a new sun. Trust your feminine energies—
> creativity, intuition and imagination. These will add
> new sunshine to your life. Don't be afraid to roar if
> you feel threatened or intruded upon.

The next morning after walking Bailey, I head to Vee's Place.
Walking in, I find her at the dining room table. She has rebounded
and so have I.

"Well, the lioness roared!" I exclaim before taking a seat across
from her at the table.

Vee is beaming a new light. *How does this happen?* In front of
her, a white Haviland china plate holds the remains of scrambled
eggs. "What's happening?" she asks, breaking off a chunk of dark
chocolate from a small dish in the center of the table.

"You're not going to believe this, but I had a dream last night
about a lioness. So I looked up the meaning of lion in *Animal-Speak*.
The last line read, "Don't be afraid to roar if you feel threatened or
intruded upon.""

"Well, you certainly roared!"

We sit for a few minutes before I apologize. She doesn't think
anything more about it, which is so my mom. We enter a new day,
and I am grateful to be back at my daily chores. After changing
her sheets, and leaving half a marijuana cookie and banana on her
nightstand, I close the blinds. She will consume both should she
experience pain on waking from her nap. I watch as she climbs in

between her pink flannel sheets to practice the art of dying. Three hours later, from her living room, I hear her gasping for air. She struggles for a few minutes and then settles into a normal breathing pattern.

"Are you okay?" I ask.

"Oh, yes, but I think I stopped breathing again."

Chapter Seven

Where Is Dave Barry?

The universe has just granted me a huge break. My mother knew about it and told me to call John Moreland, that he had a surprise for me. I'm not up for surprises and I'm feeling frazzled. Hesitantly, I call John and learn that an anonymous person donated a full pass to the 2014 Sun Valley Writers' Conference, asking that it "to go to a writer who has had a tough year". I have been chosen.

So here it is, the first day of the Sun Valley Writers' Conference. I've laid out my outfits for all four days according to the weather forecast. Recently, I haven't given my daily wardrobe much thought, such a minor detail in the scheme of things. I feel good, very good. I've printed the program and pre-planned all my sessions. This year's theme resonates with me. The title of the conference is *Stories We Tell*. Registration and a no-host bar are from 4:30-6:00 p.m. on the resort's upper green. I plan to arrive right around 4:30. Then I will go for a glass of wine and mingle with the 1500 guests before heading to the Pavilion for the opening with Dave Barry and Ridley

Pearson. The title of their presentation is "Two Guys, One Story: A Mermaid Wouldn't Say That."

I leave my place in Hailey and begin the short drive to Sun Valley. Turning right on Dollar Road, I follow the rest of the cars into a dirt parking lot. A man signals where to park, and I exit and start heading in the direction of the Pavilion. I'm still not sure exactly what I'm supposed to do or where to get my pass, but it doesn't matter. Soon I will be enjoying a glass of wine, joining other writers for this year's kick-off. Walking alone near a roped-off section, I find a woman with a clipboard.

"Hi, I'm not sure where to go," I say.

"Oh here," she says lifting the rope. "Follow me."

We head towards a small line of people when someone hands me a champagne flute filled with ice cold bubbly. A woman fashionably dressed, carrying a champagne flute, approaches me and exclaims, "I love your outfit!" We become instant best friends. Before I know it, I'm moving along in a line of people towards a bus. Everyone climbs aboard, champagne flutes in hand. My new friend and I find the last two available seats in the back of the bus. She talks all the way to where the bus stops at Dollar Mountain Lodge. I disembark completely confused. *Is this the upper green?* The bus unloads while the driver cheers everyone on. I follow the small stream of guests as they find their places in line at the welcome table. I move towards "R" for Riley. For some reason, they can't find my name anywhere.

"Well, my ticket was a gift, so I'm wondering if it's under the donor's name."

"What's that name?"

"I don't know. It was an anonymous donor."

"Come with me," a woman says. As we reach the doors to the lodge, she tells one of the women to go ahead and place a band on my wrist and then takes off back to the crowded check-in table. I meet my friend and head inside. People are there to greet us and exchange our champagne flutes with etched wine glasses. Everyone is so friendly and cheerful, such a gala event. I look around. *Where is Dave Barry?*

Some of the wines being poured are my favorites from when I lived in California. What a treat. It's much finer wine than I normally drink. I mingle with the guests and chat with wine experts. Eventually my new friend and I head outdoors and find tables filled with gourmet hors d'oeuvres from local restaurants. I see a group of people starting to set up beach chairs over on the lawn. *Oh maybe that's where Dave Barry will be.* A couple walks up to the table where we are standing and without saying a word set their plates down.

"I can't believe you didn't bid on that dinner for six!" The woman stares at her man, clearly upset.

"I thought it was dinner for four."

The conversation between them continues while my brain tries to comprehend a bid of $50,000. I stand before them completely dumbfounded. With just under $5 to my name, eating on borrowed money, and witnessing my mother prepare for her death, here I am at this gala event watching a couple argue about why he didn't bid on a $50,000 dinner for six. I choke on a piece of arugula about the time I realize I am clearly at the wrong event. Dave Barry was somewhere else in Sun Valley, probably already on stage at the Pavilion, entertaining a sold-out crowd for this year's writers' conference. And here I am in the midst of some of the wealthiest people on earth. I did not purchase a ticket for *this* event.

Feeling guilty, I excuse myself, head back inside, put my wine glass down and quickly thank all the happy people working near the doors. When someone says the glass is for me to keep, I graciously decline the offer. A gentleman opens the door for me and compliments me on my outfit. Thanking him, I bolt to where the bus is parked, and board with giddiness. The driver exclaims, "You're leaving early!"

"Yes, and I had such a grand time!"

Riding the bus back down to the parking lot, I still can't believe what has just happened. The fact that I had several compliments about my outfit makes me smile even more because I am wearing the same outfit I wore to my husband's funeral in 1999, fifteen years ago.

It wasn't until the next morning that I realize last evening's event was the annual fundraiser for The Sun Valley Center for the Arts. Smiling at the thought of crashing this exclusive fundraiser, I prepare for a new day full of speakers. Arriving for the first session in the Pavilion, I'm excited but still feel a bit on edge about attending last night's event. Somehow I end up in the men's room facing a line of urinals and nearly panic when men start exiting the stalls. Two young boys stand paralyzed, looking at me like I have two heads. News hit the local paper the following week indicating that The Sun Valley Center for the Arts had raised over one million dollars for the three-day event. I'm not sure what the ticket price was for my evening of exclusive wine tasting, but I do know I needed a break. My mother is absolutely delighted when I tell her.

PART II

The Deepening

"To successfully move forward on the pathway of uncertainty, having patience is not optional. Patience *is* the portal to what is next. Patience is far more than just a virtue. It is the way."

Dr. Dennis Merritt Jones
Author, *The Art of Uncertainty*

Chapter Eight

Many Messengers

Vee is in quite a bit of pain all day. She is sleeping more now, and her breathing is beginning to change. I make arrangements for Bailey and spend another night with Vee. After making my bed on the floor in the living room, I lie down wondering how long this will go on. Vee seems to move in and out of end-of-life breathing, commonly known as Cheyne-Stokes. For now, as I stare up through the large paned glass window at Pyramid Mountain, it seems Vee's struggle has temporarily ceased.

I'm awakened abruptly at 4:02 a.m. by a gasp. There is a momentary sensation of not knowing where I am, but I quickly recover. Climbing out of my makeshift bed, I approach her bedroom door slowly. *Will I be able to handle this?*

"This is getting ridiculous!" In the glow of the salt lamp, I see she is rolling her eyes at me. Her thin body barely rises under the pink flannel blanket. I have no words to console her. It just is.

"Can you bring me half a banana and half a cookie?"

"Yes."

I watch as she chews mindfully. It's been a practice of hers for as long as I can remember. She shoots a glance at the ceiling as if looking for a message or messenger. "The faces are beginning to appear again. They cover the entire ceiling."

"Do you recognize any of them?"

"No."

Vee sleeps soundly most of the morning. Realizing that I may now be spending more and more time at Vee's Place, I contact my neighbor, Terry, who is more than happy to take care of Bailey. I wonder how I will ever thank her.

Crawling back into my make-shift bed, I listen as my mother's breathing fluctuates according to her body's process. Despite my exhaustion, I turn the portable CD player on and listen to David Whyte's *What To Remember When Waking* CD; I hear what I need to hear. Whyte encourages one to open up a relationship with the unknown and not to begin asking questions that cannot be answered. I like that. Besides, death is a vulnerable place, and it happens to be on the map whether it's you who is dying or whether you're involved in the end-of-life care for another. We will all take that detour. And, while walking out on the dying field, beside my mother, I find myself creating a new way of being. I'm getting back in touch with the *knowing* part of my soul. The more I open, the more I remember.

I'm awakened mid-day by another sound. Vee shuffles across the hardwood floor towards the kitchen. "Did you get some rest?" I ask.

"Yes, but I am hungry."

"What can I get you?"

"I don't know."

Stepping up from the living room, I find her standing in the kitchen, hands in the pockets of her blue robe. Her gray hair is matted and standing straight up. "I think I'll take a sponge bath, get cleaned up."

I prepare lunch and reflect more on David Whyte's message. Peeking into Vee's room, I notice she is applying her favorite Clinique moisturizing cream in upward swipes along the sides of her face. She has changed clothes and is wearing one of her favorite scarves.

"Lunch is ready."

"Oh good. I'll be right out." The mood has shifted. She almost seems back in her normal state.

Over lunch, I ask her whether she would be willing to do more interviews.

"What do you mean?" She shoots me a look, one of curiosity.

"I was thinking it would be cool to interview you on my phone. Make a short video of you talking about what it's like to die a conscious death."

"Well, alright," she says calmly.

I marvel at the opportunity of capturing my mother on video while she speaks openly about dying:

"Hi, I'm sitting here talking to Kate. And the wind is blowing. I'm listening to the wind chimes because one day, when I was on a walk about five months ago, before I was feeling bad… I'm not feeling bad at all times but sometimes I feel like I'm getting closer to dying. And so that's what I was going to talk about. But I want to mention the wind chimes because when I was on my walk, I asked the mountain, Pyramid Mountain, how much longer I had to live, and the mountain said, 'Listen to the wind'. Well, it's been several months and how am I going to listen to the wind? I can see that the wind is blowing, but I don't feel as though I am listening to it. So last night, I had a wonderful experience. I was lying in my bed, and Kate had pulled the shades down, and the sun was shining through them. I was seeing shadows, beautiful, beautiful movement

43

of the shadows, and I said, 'This is listening to the wind!' So that was my experience last evening. And that was beautiful. Also, I felt I was getting really close to dying. I have felt this two or three times, but it's a strange experience because you think you're getting close and then you don't die. I mentioned to Kate that if you think you have made up your mind to die, it would be so easy to do, because I have cleared many, many things. I don't think there is anything else I need to clear. Whatever happens after I die, the people will have to deal with that. It is not my responsibility anymore to take care of things. I have a beautiful flower garden here, and so I'm enjoying myself, but as far as it being easy to die..."

NEXT SEGMENT

"You would think it would be very easy to die if you had made up your mind and had given yourself permission to die. I don't know what else there is to do. That's why I think it's really important for people to know if they're going to be involved in death and dying that it's not easy. I want to remain conscious. I don't want to take anything that is going to make me unconscious because I want to be present for the whole experience. As long as I can do that, I will be happy."

Vee spends the latter part of the afternoon sitting on her front porch. She tells me the birds are starting to come around more. "I love watching them splash in the bird bath," she exclaims. We share popcorn and a little Chardonnay, and then she excuses herself. I find her settling into her bed for the night. I take a seat next to her.

"Kate, in all your speaking engagements, please say, 'It's not easy dying'."

I feel her struggle, yet there is nothing I can do but hold space. She has already spoken these words several times. I rise from her bed to close the blinds.

"I'm not checking out because I don't want to be here. I'm checking out because I know it's my *time*. And, after I die, call Anna and Sara and tell them I *just slipped away*. Will you say that?"

"Yes."

"Anna will call all the relatives."

"Oh good; that's really not something I want to do."

"She'll be good at it!" Smiling, she closes her eyes.

I head for my makeshift bed on the living room floor. Staring up through the large window, I share my discomfort with Pyramid Mountain. *How is it that family members separate during the death of a loved one?* Closing my eyes, I wonder why my sisters never responded to my invitation.

Chapter Nine

The Eye of God

Entering Vee's bedroom, I detect another shift. The energy is very different. Her hands are folded across her chest, her body motionless. The blinds are still closed, and it feels like something lurks in the shadows.

"I am seeing the eye of God again. I believe I'm getting closer and closer to moving through."

Startled by her voice, I look at her ceiling and search for clues. As in prior situations, when the dying are describing something to me—something that is taking place in their rooms—I search in hopes of getting a glimpse into their world. The dying are privy to details and scenes that we simply cannot perceive. Nonetheless, I always inquire and then draw my own conclusion based on what they've described. Mostly, I'm left only with an image that comes from my untamed imagination. Glancing Vee's way, I ask whether she needs anything. She shakes her head and closes her eyes. The surrendering is an ongoing process. I admire her courage and her stamina and am enamored with her perseverance.

Leaving her be and going outside, I ponder this eye of God thing. Perhaps some of the ensuing difficulty in getting through the eye of God is losing the *I* – in other words freeing herself from the ego and the illusion of separateness in order to move through and become totally one with what lies beyond. Lying in the damp grass, I meditate on the cumulus clouds moving overhead, the large masses building one upon another on a flat base. I can't help wondering whether Vee is looking at something similar. What would it take for me to move up through the cloud, disappearing into the light? Continuing to rest in the quiet of a new day, I give thanks. Such a humbling experience to witness my mother's dying. Off in the distance I hear children laughing. Now and then a dog barks. Two large ravens swoop in and land on the ridge of my mother's roof. They look to be the same two that come and go. Something tells me to head back inside, where I find Vee in the same exact position, hands folded ever so tenderly over her heart.

"I continue to move towards the eye of God. It's no longer oval, but round and flat." I think about the cumulus clouds above. "It even has lashes. So, I plan to meditate nonstop because I believe all I need to do is move through the eye. It's God, Kate."

As she closes her eyes again, I'm left standing bedside with nothing to say. After a few moments, her eyes open. I watch as she begins to scan the ceiling above her bed.

"There is some kind of writing on the ceiling. I keep seeing white writing on yellow, like faded newspaper print."

Glancing upward, I find nothing. "Is there a date?" I ask, half kidding.

"No, I can't seem to make out the words, but they're there."

My mother closes her eyes. Unsure about things, I leave her resting. She seems comfortable, especially with the eye of God. I read and journal most of the afternoon. It feels very much like we're both in a holding pattern, periodically receding into our own worlds. A few hours later, Vee exits her bedroom.

"I've been thinking about ways to leave this world." My mother stands, weakened. A wrinkled tissue spills out of her sleeve. I watch as she shuffles slowly across the hardwood floor. On one hand, I desperately want to know her thoughts. On the other hand, no, I'd rather not. This is not a conversation I am prepared to have, now or anytime soon.

Later, I prepare her bedroom in the usual manner, raising the blinds and opening the windows for fresh air. I change the water in the ultrasonic diffuser and ask which essential oils she would like. She leaves that up to me. Taking a vase of wilted flowers into the kitchen, I make a mental note to pick up some fresh roses the following day. I cut a banana in half and place it on a small Haviland saucer and take a marijuana cookie from the freezer. Splitting it in half, I think how nice it would be to eat one or maybe five or six, but I can't. As I place the two small plates on her nightstand, she requests music. After a moment, she decides on *Sophia*. When I open the CD case, I notice Sophia has written a personal message to Vee. The title is *Return*.

"Do you need anything else, Mom?"

"No thank you. I hope you get some rest tonight."

"You, too."

As I lower the blinds, the chorus on the CD sings: *Return from the darkness. Forward to the light.*

"I love you, Mom."

With eyes closed, she gives me a quick flick of her wrist and then folds her hands across her chest. I leave for home, trusting Vee's soul to steer her in the right direction. She is clearly headed into the eye of God.

Chapter Ten

The Verdict

The dying process continues in much the same way for the next month. As Vee sticks to her daily practice in the art of dying, I commit to my new practice: the art of being. Waiting for death to arrive is starting to weigh heavily despite my vow to remain my mother's caregiver to the end.

Arriving at Vee's Place, I head up the walkway to find her sitting in the white wicker chair on her front porch. She's in a meditative mood and says she's been watching the blackbirds bathing in the birdbath. Her hands are folded in her lap. It's happy hour, but there is no glass of wine on the small wicker table next to her. I skip past her and leave a bowl of hot chicken on the kitchen counter, hoping she will eat it. My plan is to dart out of there and drive to Ketchum and pick up the book I placed on hold, *The Death of Ivan Ilyich*, by Tolstoy (1886). Roshi Joan Halifax claims there is a dying scene that is one of the most moving scenes she has ever read. Deep down in my heart, I yearn to write a beautiful scene, one in which my mom dies a beautiful death, a scene that moves people, opens people and helps shift old worn-out perceptions based on fear, opening people to plan for a good death ahead of time. Hesitantly, I head back to Vee's front porch. She seems pensive. Something is going on, and I'm not sure I want to know.

I study her up close and notice she seems irritated. Once again, I sense she doesn't want to be here anymore. I pull up the red foot stool next to her.

"Did you see my note?" she asks.

"Yes, something about the dryer."

"You keep putting the dial over to the right, and it's not drying the wash," she says annoyed. "Maybe you better go place the wet clothes in the dryer."

"Okay." Rising, I find myself getting agitated. The library closes in 45 minutes and I will have to wait until Monday if I don't make it in time. I am desperate to read about a good death. Turning the dryer dial to the correct position, I head back out and take a seat on the red stool.

My mother looks at me and says, "I'm thinking about stopping food and water. Maryanne's mother says it will take three days."

I stare directly into my mother's eyes. *You can't be serious.* In silence, I begin to realize the ultimatum of her remark.

"Well, what if it takes longer than three days?" My fear surfaces as an uninvited guest.

"I don't have much body mass."

"Yeah, Louise took longer because she was heavy and her leg..." I drop off. Nothing I am saying is relevant. Besides, I find myself more preoccupied with the library closing.

"I'm not drinking any wine tonight."

I understand her plan but am not sure I want to be a part of it.

"Okay, I'll drop your groceries off after I get back from Ketchum."

"If I do this, I will have a nurse come in for the three days."

"Okay, sounds good." *What?!*

"I will call hospice..."

"Maybe you should talk to Rosemary directly."

"That's a good idea," she says as she gets up and carefully passes through her front door. I follow her back inside.

"I want you to cash another check and put the money here." I watch as she points to her small green trunk. "You guys are going to need some cash on hand."

"Okay, will do. I'm going to Ketchum now."

"Thank you for the chicken."

"I hope you eat some for dinner, Mom."

"I will."

We hug and say, "I love you" to each other. I leave my dark glasses on through the exchange. Pulling out of her driveway, it hits me. *God! Is she really going to do this?!*

As I head north through town, a faded red Chevrolet beater crosses into my lane. I look over at the 20-something young woman and despise her. Underneath it all, I despise being a part of my mother's decision, even though it's not final. She is probably going to go through with it. And what this means is, I will be there for the days it takes, watching my own mother starve herself so that she can die. And if it takes three days, or five or seven, I will be there waiting, watching, and hurting. The hourglass turned upside down one last time. Will I be able to feed her ice chips when needed—not too much, just enough to moisten her parched lips? How long will it take her kidneys to shut down? Will the nurse be able to tell me what's going on at every stage? Will there even be a nurse? Will I be able to support my mother's decision or will I end up begging her not to go? Will I weep uncontrollably at her bedside or go outside and wail in her meditation garden while the blackbirds cover her lawn and the ravens take to her rooftop?

Retrieving my book, I suppress thoughts of lying with my mom while she disappears into the light. Tears blur my vision, but I'm carried back to Hailey where I wander aimlessly through the aisles of the local grocery store picking up half-and-half, sharp cheddar cheese, and organic Columbian coffee for my mom, who may or may not decide to open them. I drop the few items off quickly, open all her windows in the event she does die, and head for home where I don't want to be either. Holland is here for the night. I want to be someplace where I have no responsibilities, a place where someone will take care of me, feed me dinner, a place where I don't have to make a decision on the meal, and then cook it, and clean up afterwards. Maybe I should go out and order my mom's favorite french fries and a glass of Pinot Noir, where I can sit at the bar, trying not to think of helping my mom die in this way.

Exhausted, I drop onto the bed in our spare room. I've clearly stepped out of the dance both with my partner and my mom. How can I dance in the mystery while I now know that my mom has an allotted time left, possibly as short as three days? Will she begin the ultimate fast tomorrow morning? I feel an unwanted sense of urgency. Soon my mother will take her last breath.

The following morning, I walk Bailey and pass my post box on the way back. I find a small mailer situated snugly inside. Opening it immediately, I read the cover. "#1 New York Times Bestseller, *FINAL EXIT - The Practicalities of Self-Deliverance and Assisted Suicide for the Dying*," written by Derek Humphry. A friend had suggested I read it. One review reads, "Straightforward…speaks to a growing concern of most Americans" - Newsweek. At the top printed inside a gold seal: Third Edition Revised and Updated! Walking, I open the book randomly. My eyes fall on four pencil sketches on page 134. The title at the top of the page reads, "The EXIT bag and helium technique." Slamming the book shut, I proceed home with Bailey where I toss the book on the windowsill next to my writing table. I want nothing to do with any of it.

I leave for Vee's Place and find a car in the driveway. *Oh good! This must be the nurse.* Watering Sean's little tree, I wonder whether my mom has died. Then I hear a car door shut. Walking over, I smile. The nurse puts her window down. She tells me Vee is doing fine. I bring up the recent radio program on death with dignity. She tells me she had listened to the program as well. Curious, I ask what she thought of the conversation. As she begins to convey her disagreement, my blood pressure begins to rise. I listen as she continues to explain that she would want to make the person comfortable by administering drugs. I counter immediately. "Even when people are very clear and ready to die?" I ask, annoyed.

"No, we would want to keep the person comfortable, and we could administer drugs."

"So, you don't think that the drugs in this situation could actually cause more agony and a prolonged death?

"Yes, but I would suggest making arrangements to make them comfortable," she reiterates.

"But what if they don't want to be comfortable? What if they want *TO DIE*, then what?"

"I don't know," she says defeated.

Our conversation is clearly at odds and going absolutely nowhere. As she backs out of the driveway, I wave goodbye. Walking across the backyard, I struggle with the intensity of what just happened and question my ability to head into my mother's decision.

Chapter Eleven

The Long Debut

"Kate, I've decided to move forward with my plans," my mother announces.

Her words come as no surprise. I had been processing everything since she'd first told me of her plans. I'm now at that juncture and feel as if I've reached some level of acceptance. I'm not sure how I got here.

"Mom, I need to ask you something. Are you okay with morphine if there is pain on dehydration? Also, how will you let me know you are in pain, if you become delirious?"

"I would rather die without morphine. You know this already. Why you felt the need to order it at the end of May, I will never know. It's remained on my nightstand all this time, unopened," she says, annoyed.

"I simply wanted to have some on hand. You were in a lot of pain while I was presenting at the wellness festival." I want to tell her it was Susan's idea, but then decide against it. My mother gets up and slowly shuffles across her room. The conversation has ended.

I wonder if she is planning on it all happening quickly. I feel caught in no-mans land. How does one prepare for something like this? Later in the evening, we have a glass of wine and talk. She tells me that when she fell asleep earlier, she woke and couldn't open her eyes. "I knew I had been somewhere, and then when my eyes opened, I thought, *Did I just die?*" One of her favorite songs, by Pink Martini, *Que Sera Sera*, plays in the background. It all feels surreal again.

Waking the following morning, I receive a call from Sean. He is in Scotland. He said he was experiencing an overwhelming need to fly home. He was booking a ticket for the next flight out and would let me know his itinerary later.

When I arrive at Vee's Place late morning, she asks for a mimosa. We take our champagne flutes outside to the Riley bench on her front porch. It feels like a celebratory time. She is delighted to hear the news about Sean flying back home. We toast and watch the birds gather round. Then she tells me she wants me to have her parents' rocking chair and shares with me its history. Teary-eyed, she speaks about how her mother and dad both sat in it, and decided on adding the wooden rockers later. She thought they purchased the chair in 1925 or 1926 when they were married. "My dad used to swing a leg over the arm of the chair. He rocked all the kids in it and would sing to us."

We continue the conversation, which leads to a discussion of items inside her home. I mention the things I would cherish and then question whether or not Anna and Sara would want them.

"Oh, Sara probably doesn't have room for much!"

"Don't assume anything, Mom."

"Okay."

"Why don't you call them again and ask?" I suggest.

"Okay, I'll call before my afternoon treatment with Maryanne. Maybe if I tell them I'm starting to give things away, they will speak up."

"Good idea."

While Vee has her treatment, I lie down under the birch tree and stare up at my favorite scene in the sky, white cumulus clouds spanning across expansive blue skies. I'm dizzy and completely drained and wonder how long this is all going to take. In the meantime, I must find ways to remain in the present moment with her—it's so much easier that way. Walking back inside, I find my mother still on her massage table. It's obvious she has thoroughly enjoyed her treatment.

"John is waiting for me and he informs me that he has a new joke, one that I haven't heard before."

I laugh. The whole family had been subject to my father's endless jokes and repeated storytelling right up to the moment an ICU nurse placed a ventilator tube into his windpipe.

"I've heard them all!" Vee exclaims.

My mother is radiant. There is a transparency about her now.

"This conscious dying is a pretty neat thing. I'm seeing lots of vivid colors and there are different levels." She attempts to show me with her hand, motioning up from her throat area and moving up above her head. I notice her own eyes shine brightly with a radiant light. "There are all these eyes behind one larger eye. A form of some kind, a Supreme being."

After a brief pause, she lets me know she wants to remain on her table for awhile, alone.

Settling into my grandparents' rocker, I begin the book, *Imperfect Endings: A Daughter's Tale of Life and Death,* by Zoe Carter Fitzgerald. When I get to page 30, I read, "Once my mother's damaged neurotransmitters were left to their own devices, she would temporarily shut down, entering a state akin to a waking coma, with little or no ability to move."

"Oh My God!!" My head drops back and lands on the crest of the padded rocking chair. I stare at the ceiling fan and contemplate unwanted thoughts. *What if my mom does move forward with her plan and she falls into a comatose state?* This is something I can't handle, I'm already at the edge. But I continue reading. I put the book down four chapters later after reading, "Closing my eyes, I imagine my mother lying in her bed, lonely and afraid. Not of death, but of the long, ugly road leading to death. And because I'm her daughter, both by birth and by design, I'm trapped on that road with her until one of us, or perhaps both of us, can engineer her release."

Taking in a huge long breath, I feel a sharp stabbing pain in the left side of my chest. *Oh God, maybe I'll die first.*

The next day, Vee tells me she wants to do something else with the bed. I have exhausted all possibilities. I have moved mattresses and beds, ordered a hospital bed, had plywood cut to fit under the thick mattress, and then called the pharmacy to have the hospital bed picked up for return. She has been very uncomfortable since she sold the 1800s spindle bed she'd slept in for decades. But the bed was high off the floor, and it was getting more and more difficult for her to climb into. I was also concerned she might fall out in the night. Now I wonder whether she really wanted to sell it. The money helped to pay her property tax bill for six months, but had she really wanted to give it up? I will never know.

Despite my exhaustion at making every attempt to ensure her comfort, nothing seems to be working. My physician friend, Michael, tells me Vee's rib cage is most likely caving in from the loss of support due to multiple fractures from metastatic bone lesions. I'm hoping to find the perfect remedy. As a last resort, Holland and I end up delivering our own king size mattress. He sets up the bed frame without using the box springs so the mattress is closer to the floor for easier access. I am beside myself, and hope to God this remedies her current dilemma.

***

It's August 15, eight months since the appointment with Dr. Kastner. My mother seems depressed. Under normal circumstances, medication might be offered, but she won't have anything to do with it. I surprise her with fresh halibut for dinner, but she barely eats. She remains in bed more these days and claims to be practicing her dying. When I crawl in next to her, our bare feet side by side against the foot rail, she tells me it's comforting to have me nearby. Her eyes are closed and I begin to sync my own breath with hers. Music is playing in the background. I believe it is *Sophia*, the CD she has chosen for the moment she dies. I lie there for a long time as evening turns to night. Everything is lifted, as if life and death—in the space between here and there—have given us pause.

As the days pass and my mother approaches her final exit, tensions rise between Sara and me. It can't be easy living so far away. In the meantime, Anna tells me she is walking the mall, that it feels good to exercise. I would give anything to be walking the mall and I think malls are disturbing places. I suppose it's time to go it alone, but I desperately need help. During intermittent spells of feeling overwhelmed, somehow I find moments to relax into the care of Vee in a different light. One soul aiding another soul who is ready to leave—a noble act really. If only I could remain in this higher vibration. I seem to flit up and down, in and out.

Anna informs me she will be arriving next week to use the pedicure gift certificate from mom, adding that she'll be bringing a Heavenly Ham. "So feel free to come to moms to munch ham!" *What?* As Anna leaves her home, we speak briefly on the phone. Before she hangs up, she reiterates, "I will not be spending the night." She seems tense, and I realize she, too, is *waiting* for the end. It's never easy. I phone Sara. She tells me she can't get away, "There's too much going on here." And then she genuinely thanks me. This is all I need.

The next morning, while lying in my own bed, I notice my nervous system feels on high alert. I remember this same feeling during the years it took for my husband to die and the weeks for my father. You wait and wait and death doesn't come. As Vee has maintained all along, "You cannot push death!"

I skip my coffee and head to Vee's Place where I find her in bed unable to move. She is in excruciating pain. "I think it's just a muscle, Kate." She tells me she can no longer do the things she is used to doing. "Yesterday, I tried to lift the tea kettle and it was too heavy."

Taking a seat on the edge of her bed, I reflect on what Michael said about her rib cage. My heart aches, and I'm unsure whether or not to share the information with her. I question whether the marijuana cookies will continue to help reduce the pain if fractures become more frequent. For now, we sit in the silence.

Things are changing quickly.

PART III

The Quickening

"Dying wise is a thought unthought—a rumor—in a culture
that does not believe in dying, and it will take about as much courage
and wisdom as you can manage to do it. Dying wise is a life's work.
Dying wise is the Rhythm, the Story, around which human life must swirl."

Stephen Jenkinson
Author, *Die Wise: A Manifesto for Sanity and Soul*

Chapter Twelve

Plan Vee: On Her Own Terms

"Well, Kate. It's time to move from Plan A to Plan B." I wait patiently to hear the details despite having a good sense of what the new plan might entail. A wrinkled white Kleenex tissue spills out of the right sleeve of my mother's pink terrycloth robe, and in the silence my thoughts take me to her washer. Everyday for months, I have picked out tiny pieces of shredded tissue clinging to the inside of the washing machine. One day, I will miss this small meditative deed. We sit in the quiet space of her sanctuary. It's the first time she's been in her living room for quite some time. The large Buddha statue faces us, smiling. A warm breeze blows in from the open windows.

"I'm closing in on myself. I don't want to become handicapped. My leg has a new sore and the other sores are bleeding. My skin is peeling off. Kate, I'm shedding my earthly body." She smiles like a small child. "When I ask Pyramid, the mountain says 'Wait a little bit longer.' Maryanne is coming over this afternoon and I plan to tell her I've come to the end of my rope." A long pause ensues and, with it, recognition. We both know what's coming. Several western tanagers convene on the birch tree outside Vee's living room window, feeding on the hanging seed socks Anna had gifted her. I wait in silence. "I feel good. I've been happy over the past fourteen years. But, I am at the end of my life. And, I have to admit, I'm falling in love with my future." She smiles. I feel reasonably sure she wants me to feel good with respect to her final decision. Fourteen years have gone by since she discovered the malignant breast tumor. And here we are now clearly at the end of her life. Nothing has really changed in the interval as far as how Vee approaches the end of her life. She continues to weigh all her options carefully—despite there being only a few—maintaining her autonomy to the very end.

"As soon as our hospice meeting is over, I will call Anna. I will also call Nick and see about getting him here sooner. Besides, he did tell me the last time we spoke that he would be willing to come over anytime as long as he had enough time to get replacements for his home health care patients. I think it will go faster if he is in the other room. And I would like for him to have Buddha." After a long pause, she says, "I'm ready to throw in the towel!"

The doorbell rings and startles both of us. It's Rosemary, executive director of hospice. The three of us sit at the dining room table where we discuss various options. Vee has, however, clearly made up her mind. She no longer needs to discuss options, even for treatment or pain relief. We both know that the marijuana cookies are helping with the pain, and she intends to quietly stay with her plan. I wonder whether or not she will give up the cookies when she decides to stop eating. Vee is tired and goes to lie down; the conversation wears her out. I see Rosemary to the front door.

I listen as Cheyne-Stokes breathing begins again. Part of me wants Vee to stop breathing on her own and never have to go through the starvation process. I think about how she had recently said, "I just don't like the word, *suicide*." I had stoically responded, "Well, maybe we could change the language." Listening to long periods of shallow breathing with intermittent sudden gasps for air is not something one gets accustomed to. This has been going on for quite some time and even today, knowing what's coming, I'm unsettled. I try to remain busy cleaning the kitchen and doing her laundry, but I'm fatigued and sleep deprived. Opening her dryer door even takes enormous effort on my end.

Later in the afternoon, I watch as my mother painfully endures baby steps across the hardwood floors, her white hair matted down in the back. As she takes a seat at the dining room table, I ask if she will read aloud the epilogue she wrote for *The Green Velvet Journals* (which she and I co-authored in 2004). Her message at that time seems pertinent to where she is fourteen years later. She says she will give it her best shot, but I sense she is done with life. Retrieving a copy of our book, I hand it to her opened to the epilogue. She begins clearing her throat while I get my cell phone to record her. After a few attempts, I realize it's simply too much for her, and we end the recording session.

Vee requests that we sit on the front porch. Plan B is renamed Plan Vee. My mind follows along as my mother graciously baptizes me with the details. "I called Nick and he assures me he will stay with me to the very end." In a way, knowing the decision has been made from a place of clarity, I will not be alone in the plan that will end my mother's life. Vee is competent and I don't question her decision.

"Mom, will you give me advanced notice?" The more warning I have, the better equipped I will be emotionally, I think. As Vee prepares, so must I. She supports me and I wonder whether I will have the courage to get through it. My involvement will simply be to continue loving her, caring for her, getting her whatever she needs in the way of washcloths or ice chips, lip balm, tissues, and whatever else to make her comfortable. Changing the water in the diffuser twice daily and adding essential oils has become routine. Closing her window blinds may occur more often now and adding blankets for warmth as her body begins to shut down. I suppose we have come to the denouement of my mother's narrative. Once again, this is *her* story. Her life. Standing by, I must allow her to dictate how it ends.

"Kate, get a piece of paper and a pen. I have a story to write." I head inside and retrieve a tablet and pen. "Okay, shoot!"

Living here in the beautiful Wood River Valley, my home for the last decade, I sense the door is about to close on my life. Sitting in the white wicker chair on my front porch, once again I am entertained by nature. Watching the Blackbird in the bird bath as it splashes water crystals through the air brings joy and pure delight. Diving from willow branch to lilac bush it continues moving toward the sky like a little jet. I am filled with wonder. Will my flight into the unknown be as simple and smooth? Engaging in an inner awareness, I experience the presence of perfection in the universal whole.

Maryanne arrives and they go into the treatment room where Vee lies down on her massage table. I hear my mother telling Maryanne she has come to the end of her rope. And then I think about Vee wanting to die right there on her massage table, such a central part of her life work. I hope it happens for her in this way. The door to the massage studio closes gently. As Maryanne begins the treatment, I head back outside.

The entire lawn surrounding Vee's home is host to flocks of blackbirds. I watch as they tiptoe around, cock their black shiny heads in unison, listening for grubs beneath the grass. I question whether they *know* something. Have they arrived to assist? Reflecting on a prior trip to the library to pick up Wallace Stevens first book of poetry for my mom, I wonder now whether she gleaned anything from his poem, "Thirteen Ways of Looking at a Blackbird"? Robins begin arriving and crowd the birdbaths for a cool drink, splashing about content and carefree. Will they help lift her to the castle in the sky? The front door is wide open, and I wonder whether they will enter into this sacred space. The mood is especially serene. Quiet prevails, while I lie down amongst the birds and watch the usual display of puffy white clouds move slowly across the high desert mountain skies. Ravens land on the ridge of my mother's roof; this time there are three of them.

It's only 5 p.m. as Vee prepares herself for bed, still applying Clinique moisturizing cream in upward motions. After brushing her teeth, she inches along until she reaches the side of her bed.

"What do you need, Mom?"

"How about half a banana and half a cookie?" She seems relieved, even happy, to have settled on a real plan with a start date. I place them both on her nightstand. As usual, she will take them in the night when she awakens. It seems the marijuana cookies are still helping with the pain.

"I'm so grateful I have you here and I have Nick arriving soon. I keep thinking how lucky I am." I'm speechless, mostly because her words mean the world to me. Carrying my sadness with me, I return to kitchen duty and then venture back to her room.

"Mom, what you said meant so much to me."

"What? Wait, I have to move my pillow away from my ear. I can't hear you."

"What you said tonight meant a lot to me."

"Well, I mean it!"

"I know. Sleep well."

"Okay, you, too." She closes her eyes and places both hands over her heart.

"Love you," I say as if it might be the last time.

"Love you!"

An hour later Nick arrives at the front door. I take him to my mom's bedside where they meet in person for the first time. He respects Vee's need for rest and leaves her room to begin mindfully organizing his own things in the spare bedroom where he will live until the end of my mother's life. Before leaving, I fill him in on a few details, mostly the signed POST taped to her wall just above the headboard. I also point out the list of people to call and in what order. I show him the Letter of Intent that Vee has had me type. It is signed and dated by her and will serve as a legal document should I need it. Nick seems perfectly comfortable with Plan Vee. Leaving, I feel relieved of the responsibility in planning the start date. I return home to call Sara. Realizing there is nothing more to be done, she and I both burst into tears. Mom will soon be gone.

Nick calls Anna. I'm glad to know she has the option of coming over or not.

Chapter Thirteen

Dress Rehearsal

The following morning, once I rise from my bed, I'm slow to finish my coffee and walk Bailey. Will delaying my morning ritual postpone my mother's decision to cease all foods and liquids? Something tells me today is the beginning of the end. I step into a hot shower where I yearn to remain for the rest of the morning. Dressing in recently ironed clothes, as if being with the dying is just going on with business, I slowly make my way the three blocks to Vee's Place. I'm hoping she has left in the night, relinquishing her one final breath to the moon, while under the careful watch of Nick. Walking into her home, I find my mother in bed. Nick gives me a quick update. Today is the start.

I find a handwritten note on Vee's nightstand:

> *Heaven is the decision I must make.*
> *I make it now, and will not*
> *change my mind, because*
> *it is the only thing I want.*

DAY 1 (August 28) – I lie down on my mother's bed and she opens her right eye, the one closest to me, searching.

"It's me, Mom," I whisper. She tries to speak but is unable. And then with great effort she says, "It's coming in waves," her voice husky.

"Yes, I see. Go with it," I say, noticing a significant difference from the night before.

"Ice chips," she whispers.

Moving around to the other side of the bed, I reach for the small frosted glass on the nightstand. Scooping ice chips with the tiny sterling spoon, I think about it's history. I can't help but wonder if my grandmother fed my mother with this same spoon. She takes what she needs with her tongue and then tosses them about in her mouth, her gaze now steady and fixed on me. After the ice has dissolved, she says, "Send Sean in when he gets here."

"He's on his way now. He and Holland have just left Boise."

She nods and looks away.

"Do you want me to stay with you?"

"No, it's better if I'm alone."

"Yes, I know."

My mom closes her eyes and I wonder whether she will ever look at me again. She is beautiful and brave and there is a deep peace about her now. I study her with utmost reverence. My mother has entrusted me with her death all the way to this point. The honor that comes with this is ineffable. I watch her carotid artery pulse in a thinning neck, and she opens her right eye. Her pupil moves to the right corner—I believe she is searching to see if I'm still there, on the bed next to her. I simply can't leave. She changes her mind and wants me close again. After awhile, Nick whispers from her doorway, "Sean and Holland are here." A moment later, Sean walks into her bedroom. I turn my head and acknowledge him with a smile. He smiles back and walks to the other side of the bed. We haven't seen each other since he left for Europe, but our hug can wait. Despite the two having already said their goodbyes in May, when Sean left for Spain, Grammy seems greatly relieved and she conveys it through a loving smile. They hold hands, and I watch tears float in Sean's eyes. I notice how handsome and loving he is. All she wants to do is hold hands and look at him. She attempts to speak but needs a moment to clear her parched throat.

"Is Holland here?"

"Yes, he's in the kitchen," Sean says.

"Send him in now. Tell him I want to say hello and goodbye."

"Ok, Grammy."

Holland walks in and around to her side of the bed. He is holding back the tears as he takes her hand.

"Hello, Holland."

"Hi, Vee."

It's time for me to say goodbye now."

"I love you," he says, barely holding on.

"I love you, too," she says with a knowing smile. There is a brief pause before she says, "Goodbye now."

He trembles as he struggles to say goodbye. She releases his hand, and he knows he must leave the room. I'm amazed at her candidness and ability to be so direct. There is no delay on her part. He respects her candor in spite of the intense sadness, and I watch him as he moves around the foot of her bed. By sunset, physical changes are already taking place. I'm surprised by her sunken face and realize that her jaw is already beginning to relax, possibly an early glimpse of what she might look like when she does leave. "Thank you for everything, Kate. I love having you next to me." Still so loving, her words comfort me beyond measure.

DAY 2 (August 29) - Nick is attentive, and I'm grateful to have him here. Vee reiterates that no one should ever have to do this alone. She continues to request ice chips throughout the morning. I bring her lip balm and ask whether I can apply some with a Q-tip. She loves it. I ask if it's difficult not eating, and she doesn't complain. Despite the difficulty in speaking, she is still expressing gratitude. On my way out, I show Nick the red rose bush outside the front door. One single long stem from the "Always and Forever" rises skyward. "When my mom dies, I want you to cut that one rose. I will place it over her chest in the Chariot."

DAY 3 (August 30) - I pull up in Vee's driveway and think about how my life is about to change. Going inside, I find my mom resting in her bed. She tries to talk, but it is getting more difficult. She asks what the date is. I tell her August 30th and then she closes her eyes. From the recent months, I've learned that when she gets closer to the 3rd of the month, she hangs on. My mom wants to collect every single dime possible from my father's Social Security death benefits, even if it means it will go to her three daughters. I can't imagine her living until midnight, four days from now. Sitting down at her dining room table, I take my new journal, open to the first page, and write the following passage:

> DEATH
> Dying is not easy
> even for those who
> have consciously chosen
> a good death.
>
> Despite the dying process
> in all its forms
> My mother continues
> to express gratitude.

DAY 4 (August 31st) - Vee begins to describe colors above her. Speaking requires tremendous effort and she does so slowly and methodically. Her lips are parched and cracked. I sense her entire airway is drying up, and I refrain from thinking further about this. Mostly, she uses her hands to describe the rainbow she is entering. Lying on the bed next to her, I try to envision what she is seeing. She begins to squirm as if trying desperately to get out of her body.

Then with no warning, she raises both legs high into the air and begins pedaling. She pedals faster and faster and then drops both legs onto the bed. Her prayers are audible even during moments of heartrending and mournful sobbing. She stops abruptly to say, "I'm trying to turn off my analytical mind." I can't help thinking about what it takes to die, surrendering on so many levels. I stare at the POST taped to the wall. I hear people talking in the kitchen. A loud motorbike revs in the street. I feel my world caving in from sadness and close my eyes. Tears spill onto the pink flannel sheet of my mother's bed.

Later in the afternoon, I call Susan, and she and a friend drum and sing the fire song through the speaker of my cell phone. I run the phone up and down over Vee's small body and then hand it to Nick who is bedside. Vee drops into a deep sleep. We watch her as minutes pass. She begins trembling and then sobbing again with great effort and then cries out, "Oh God! You've been so good to me!" She raises her arms straight into the air—the thin sleeves of her nightgown falling towards her shoulders, baring shriveled arms—and shakes them wildly. "Oh God, it's so hard to get out of my body!" Silence. Another soft whimper escalates into a full cry. Nick wipes her tears with his owl feather, then begins to drum ever so gently. She quiets and begins to rock back and forth. "Mom, you are so beautiful," I say lovingly. She stares at me with a sense of assuredness, unblinking in her truth to be fully with her dying process. I smile tenderly in support of her bravery. I never expected it would end like this. Leaving her room, I call Susan to tell her I think Vee is getting close. Susan will pack her things and head out for Vee's Place first thing in the morning. Nick passes me in the kitchen. "Vee wants a shot of vodka." This catches me by surprise but then think, *well, okay*. Nick helps prop Vee up against her giant yellow pillow. I lean up against the other side to help support her. Nick hands us both a shot glass. The moment feels ceremonial. Raising my glass, I catch a glimpse of our reflection in the mirrored vanity near her bed. Mother and daughter, back to back, framed in history, sipping ice-cold pellucid vodka. I breathe the timeless moment of endearment deeply in. Vee speaks softly, "I'm in a different space now."

DAY 5 (September 1) - Standing in the doorway of Vee's bedroom, I watch my mom. Her eyes are squeezed closed. She is mumbling something with conviction. And then suddenly a loud burst from her lungs, "Ahhh-ahhhh-ahhh-ahhhh!" It is one of the most beautiful voices I have ever heard. The words push up from her lungs. "Please forgive me. I forgive you. I love you. Thank you." She repeats it several times and then looks in my direction as if knowing I'm there. I take a seat on the edge of her bed where she continues singing in the most beautiful soul voice, louder and louder. Then she stops abruptly and points to the cup of ice chips on her nightstand. After feeding her a small spoonful, she rolls them around in her mouth until they melt.

Susan arrives, and although Vee is tired, she's relieved to see her. I leave them holding hands, Susan's soft voice offering loving support. After awhile, Vee requests a small amount of Chardonnay in a wine glass with a straw. Again Vee and I prop our bodies up against the large yellow pillow. I toast out loud, "Back to back, heart to heart, Mom!" And she says, "To the world I'm leaving behind!" We help Vee lie back down where she closes her eyes. Then she reaches up to tap her forehead again, "I'm still in my head." Susan calls me into the kitchen and says, "I don't think she's leaving soon, Kate."

DAY 6 (September 2) - Susan needs to return to her work but promises to drive back over the minute I call her. Vee asks, "Is everyone happy?" "Yes," I say through tears. Susan says, "Yes." Rosemary calls from hospice and asks for an update. I tell her Vee is singing a song of gratitude. Rosemary replies, "People pretty much die in character." This I believe.

Vee is requesting more ice chips, and I can't help questioning how much of these are actually hydrating her. She asks that a freezer pack be placed under her mid-back. I watch as Nick carefully places the pack under her. It's obvious she is in excruciating pain. Because my mother has stopped eating her marijuana cookies, she agrees to a small amount of morphine. I remind her what Judith had said during a recent phone call. "Remember, God is in the morphine." My mother smiles. I call and let Susan know Vee is open to a small amount of Morphine and Susan thinks this will help her body to relax. Susan's friend reminds us to allow death to call us like a lover, that the spirit needs cooperation from the body in order for it to leave. There is no pushing death. My mother begins rocking her body back and forth while Nick drums nearby. I watch as her heartbeat travels all over her chest cavity. I've never seen this before. It's almost as though her actual heart organ is free floating in a random rhythm all around the inside cavity of a chest with no rib cage seeking a viable escape route.

DAY 7 (September 3) - Vee grieves heavily her own death. My presence is not keeping her from what she, obviously, has to go through. She sobs uncontrollably, stops briefly, and then continues to weep uncontrollably. I can't help thinking about how many dying people shut down during this process out of embarrassment or simply being incapable of showing any emotion whatsoever. Yet I believe it to be an integral part of the dying process.

"Kate, I want to say one more thing," my mother speaks with enormous effort. I listen carefully as she speaks ever so slowly. "When Christ was on the cross he said seven things, and one was, 'I thirst' so now I know how he felt. I don't remember the other words. Your dad always got up on Good Friday to say those last words. I only need this one phrase because I can relate to it." She closes her eyes. I go back to my makeshift bed now set up on her bedroom floor.

Moving in and out of this world, in the space between here and there, my mother continues on through the afternoon. Once when she turns and looks at me, I sense she has been elsewhere. "Please turn on *Graceful Passages*." I turn the CD player on and she begins sobbing. "Turn it off. I need a wipe." Nick comes in and we watch as she wipes down her face. "Get me my mouthwash, please." Nick pours some in a shot glass and helps her by holding her head up, but she accidentally swallows the small amount. He is so patient with her. She rests quietly for some time while Nick and I sit outside. "Nick, maybe it's best I keep my distance…" He gets up and heads inside. I follow. "Vee, do you want to see Kate?" I watch from the door jam. She nods ever so slowly. While he motions for me to come in, she turns her head to find me. Her eyes are barely open now and her gaze is ethereal. I smile at her and begin to cry. Holding hands and exchanging loving glances is all that is left, but it's enough. "I love you, Mom." She no longer responds. Before leaving for the night, Nick and I move the Chariot onto the living room floor. I slip out while Nick hums and sings softly, "Om Shanti, Om Shanti." Something tells me my mother is loving having him close, his voice tender.

I never thought it would take my mother this long to die. To have Dr. Kastner come to her aid now would be such a gift. She had once mentioned to me how wonderful it would be to have him play his flute over her as she lay dying.

DAY 8 (September 4) - Because Vee can no longer talk, she and I stare into each other's eyes. Her green eyes have turned an opaque blue. There is no more pleading on her part, nor mine. All that is left is love. And, in this space, I have entered a state of deep peace. Death has its own agenda, its own place in the life of soul. I remain with Vee the rest of the day and wait patiently while she comes and goes between worlds. At one point she tries to convey to Nick to lift her out of bed. I'm not sure what she is asking for but Nick understands. "Do you want to stand, Vee?" She nods. This throws me a bit because she is so weak. As soon as he has her upright, pressed up against his body, she begins dropping her full weight directly onto Nick as though she is trying to shake loose from her physical body. After a few minutes she seems content and he lays her back down on the bed. She crosses her hands over her heart and stares upward. Her eyes—still soft—make me question *Why? Why is it taking so long?* Suddenly she raises her atrophied arms high into the air as if reaching out for someone she sees waiting above her. *This is harder than I thought it would be.*

DAY 9 (September 5) - Sitting bedside on the floor, I listen to my mother's breath. Her eyes are only open a fraction, and I don't think she's capable of opening them any wider. Her hands have turned bluish-purple and, if I'm not mistaken, a slight hue of the same color now surfaces on her knees. Her feet are covered with a blanket, however, I suspect the same discoloration is happening there as well. I watch as her breathing slows and then she catches her breath as if it may be her last. Lying half-clad across the bed, barely opening and closing her eyes, she and I wait for death to arrive. My mother's lifeless body and vacant stare confirm that she has entered the active dying process. And, somehow, I have cultivated courage for the moment. As promised, I lean in with her.

DAY 10 (September 6) - By late afternoon, the death rattle moves in, hoarse and raspy, a guttural roar originates at the bottom of the bronchial tube where fluid pools in stagnation. Often, invasive procedures are suggested in order to suction out the fluid. I believe this procedure is done to relieve family members more than anything. I sit on the bed next to her and listen as the roar makes its way slowly upward, the sound of a locomotive drawing closer and closer to the junction of life and death. It's a frightening sound to witness coming from your own mother. I look at the pillow next to her head. As much as I want to end her struggle, there simply isn't an ounce in me that could move forward with it. Her small head is tilted back, jaw wide open, eyes fixed on the ceiling; I struggle to hold on. Our eyes would never meet again. I rise to call hospice and then collapse on the floor next to my mother. I feel a longing so intense and so full of grief, I can hardly breathe. The death rattle seizes my mind and I glance one more time at the pillow next to her head. Rising,

I stand and lovingly tell my mother goodbye. I wave my hand over her face in case she looks into my eyes one last time. But the train is leaving the station. I turn and walk out of her bedroom. This time I don't look back.

DAY 11 (September 7) 2:30 a.m. - Nick rings my cell, "Kate, it's time to cut the red rose." Sitting up on the edge of my bed, I call Anna and Sara. "Mom...*just slipped away.*"

Chapter Fourteen

Holiness & The Final Road Trip

Arriving at Vee's Place, I pass the "Always and Forever" rose bush just outside the front door. In the glow of the porch light, I notice the long-stemmed red rose has been cut. It's 2:45 in the morning and there is a cool breeze. Advancing through the open front door, I pass Nick, my full attention focused on my mother. Picking up my pace, I head into her bedroom. As I turn to walk around the end of the bed, I am filled with enormous love. Kneeling on the edge of the mattress, I joyously shout, "Mom, you did it! We did it!"

Nick brings me a small plastic tub filled with warm water, a washcloth and a towel. I notice the white silk robe my mother had selected to wear is draped over the wrought-iron headboard. I ask Nick to bring me one of Vee's scarves, which I place under her jaw. When I bring it up over the top of her head, I realize I don't have it in me to tighten it. It feels like I will hurt her. Nick takes over, and after cinching her mouth closed says, "She looks like a little bunny rabbit." I can't help smiling.

Slowly, I begin to consecrate my mother's body, first with the bathing ritual. Nick leaves the room for me to be alone with her. Suddenly, I hear the school bell ringing outside, and I know he is announcing her passing in this way. He had asked me about the history of the school bell. When I explained it had been in our family for a long time, he asked if he could ring it outside after she passed. As I continue to lovingly wash her body, my eyes fall on her abdomen in the space between protruding hip bones. I'm overwhelmed by the power of my gratitude to her for birthing me, for loving me, and allowing me to be part of her death. After bathing her, I anoint her with essential oils she had previously selected. Starting with the crown chakra, I move down her body to her feet. I call Nick in to help me turn her over and then bathe her back. Her body suddenly looks ageless. Her legs are gorgeous, and I think about how much of a leg man my father was and then realize these legs probably had something to do with the two of them getting together. So much love floats in the room now.

"Nick, we have to carry her into the living room soon." After I finish, he grabs one end of the pink sheet and I grab the other end. God, for someone so tiny, she weighs a ton. We accidentally knock her against the door jam and I cringe. We make it to *Vee's Chariot* where we finally lower her body. In the glow of candlelight, I place the long strands of hair from each of Vee's children—starting with Sara's, then Anna's and then mine — interlacing the strands between her fingers, now cold and rigid. Nick hands me the long-stemmed red rose and I place it over my mother's chest and abdomen. The room is freezing, but Nick and I know we must keep it this way until he picks up dry ice after the store opens. He brings me a shot glass of ice cold vodka from the freezer and we toast over her body. Nick slams his. For the next three hours I sit vigil over my mother's body, slowly sipping my vodka, valiantly applauding her courageous heart and heroic decision. Charioteer Vee had done it, and in her own way. A few times it looks as though she is turning her head in my direction, but it is only my imagination. "Last night when I left you, Mom, you were already gone, weren't you?" Smiling, I reach for my cell phone and email my sisterhood who, despite being spread all over the world, have been there for me the most. The email goes out with "Vee" in the subject line; it is dated September 7, 2014, 5:22 a.m.:

A cool wind blows into this sacred space below Pyramid Mountain. Me mum so loved the rustling of aspen leaves that dance now in the moonlit sky. Candles are burning while I sit vigil next to the Chariot where she finally rests in peace. I am forever changed. In deepest gratitude, Kate

Day is beginning to break. My teeth chatter from the cold. I find Nick rolled up tightly in his down sleeping bag. Deciding not to disturb him, I head home, where I stand transfixed in the hottest and longest shower.

Returning to Vee's Place, I begin decorating the inside of the Chariot, tucking some of the long- stemmed roses, a gift from Siouxze, around my mom's body. Walking up on the hill and through the meditation garden brings back memories as I collect an assortment of wildflowers and sage. By the time I finish decorating, it truly is a work of art. I take a seat next to *Vee's Chariot* and study my mother's face. "What a courageous soul," I whisper lovingly to her.

Susan arrives and steps down into the living room. I watch as she kneels next to the Chariot. "Beautiful," she says. A few minutes pass before she informs me she has already called the funeral home. Vee is now on the docket. We will need to leave by 2:30 p.m. in order to meet the funeral director at 4:00 p.m. For a couple of hours, we walk around the house doing various things while Vee's body lies in the Chariot. I can't help checking in on her from time to time.

I call hospice, and two of the nurses stop by. One places a note inside the Chariot along with some cuttings from a house plant. Susan asks whether I should call anyone else before we begin the transport. I think about it for a moment and then call Siouxze and Alex. When Siouxze arrives, I give her the rest of the roses she had brought to Vee. "Feel free to place them in the Chariot." I start crying when I hear her drumming at my mother's side. Alex arrives and also sits with Vee. When it is time to leave, I walk into the living room where *Vee's Chariot* cradles her body. Kneeling down, I lean over and kiss her forehead and tell her I love her. When I reach for the lid to the cremation container, I can't do it. Everything so far has gone relatively well, but this act feels so final. Holding the lid to the Chariot, I struggle frantically with my emotions and collapse in despair. After a long delay, I place the lid on the container. It would be the last time I would see my mom.

Dead bodies weigh more than you think, and getting *Vee's Chariot* from the living room to the garage takes everything I have. Thank God Alex is here. When we enter the laundry room, the weight is more than I can bear. Dropping my mom's body on the linoleum floor would be catastrophic. Susan is at the foot of the Chariot and Alex is doing her best to carry the side load between the two door jams. My end is the heaviest. Just as I am about to drop my end of the Chariot, I push through with the last remaining bit of energy I have left in me. We zoom from the laundry room straight to the inside of the van, which is parked up against the laundry room door. It felt very much like we threw Vee into the van.

It takes us a few minutes to recover before leaving for the funeral home. Turning the corner onto my street, I notice two of my neighbors sitting on my front lawn. I tell Susan to honk and then decide to pull over. It's like a mini-procession cheering Charioteer Vee on! After a brief moment, we head out onto the highway.

Driving my mom's body to the funeral home is something I could not have handed over to someone else, especially a stranger.

The air conditioner in Susan's van is kaput, so we have our windows down. We aren't too concerned because Vee is packed on a small amount of dry ice. I feel free, really free, as we head south, my hair blowing wildly in the warm wind. I turn and take a photo of *Vee's Chariot* with my cell phone and send it to Anna and Sara—*Mom's last road trip.*

Arriving at the funeral home, I learn that my mom will need to spend the night in cold storage. I'm a little unsettled about this because my plan is to push the Chariot directly into the retort. I also can't imagine for a second that her body will be in a cooler. No, I didn't want this for her.

"Who knows who else is in there, Kate! Maybe she'll make some new friends," Susan says, smiling.

Her words soften my despair. Yes, my mother and I had done our work. I needed to let go of any remaining details. Running my hand over the top of *Vee's Chariot*, I turn and walk to the van. Susan and I head back out onto the highway where I stare out at the high desert landscape, the sun now beginning its descent. Arriving back in town, we go immediately to Vee's favorite restaurant for dinner. We order wine, extra bread, appetizers, entrees and desserts. Our conversation consists of three words, "Oh my God," taking turns saying it over and over. I am relieved Alex is our server. I know she understands.

The following day, Susan leaves to return home. I take Bailey to Sawtooth Animal Center for boarding. Alex picks me up and drives me to Stanley, where we enjoy a picnic on the shores of Redfish Lake followed by an overnight at Meadow Creek Inn & Spa. The massage is wonderful and sitting outside with Alex on the swing, sipping champagne, and staring off at the granite mountain range across an expansive meadow tops it all. The fact that she and I booked the reservation a long time ago, doesn't surprise me one bit. The universe had my back all along. And, this is precisely what Vee would have wanted for me.

Yes, my work is finished, and I am left with a deep reverence for both life and death. Vee had done her work here and she worked hard. That was certain. Dying is not easy. I learned that when one becomes intimate with the dying, there is a timelessness where one is elevated in the sovereignty of death. And, it was clear, I was still rejoicing in that space.

The following morning, Alex and I enjoy a leisurely drive through the Sawtooth mountain range. While unlocking my front door, I receive a text message from the funeral home. Omg, *Vee's Chariot* is now being pushed into the retort, the large green *START* button about to be hit. Simultaneously, my smoke alarm goes off. I can't help thinking my mother is letting me know. *Vee's Chariot* has been launched!

Epilogue

I believe we come into this world with a unique design, a soul signature or code. And with that comes an inner compass pointing the way with precision. Over the years, my mother taught me about instinctive energy, which is innate in all of us and works on behalf of the soul with ultimate authority. She taught me the importance of paying close attention to this compass, especially when oriented toward the heart.

As Vee bravely followed the calling of her soul home, I knew she would be capable of navigating this inner territory. I wasn't sure whether I would be able to keep up. But after accepting the invitation to lean into her death with her, I felt our souls' imprints merged, and off we danced into the great unknown, waltzing our way deep into the mystery.

Vee rocked my boat and challenged everything I thought I already knew. Dying is a private affair although shouldn't be done alone. My mother taught me what it's really like to occupy the dying field intimately with another. I think about how many people collapse on their death bed never having moved through some of the most fundamental stages of growth and transformation.

Allow death to be a great teacher. Befriend death. To be intimate with death and dying is profoundly life changing. I will never be the same.

*"There are many truths of
which the full meaning cannot
be realized until personal
experience has brought it home."*

John Stuart Mill

*"The only way to make sense out of
change is to plunge into it,
move with it, and join the dance."*

Alan Watts

A Grateful Heart

The heroine's journey is a labyrinth of twists and turns and the quest lies at the root of every story, told and untold. In this story, the entire cast contributed in profound ways. Many of you have been part of this stage crew for some time and we have spent years, decades, lifetimes practicing. Adversaries turn into allies. Silent partners have a way of becoming our greatest teachers.

To all those who helped me in better "scripting" my original manuscript, I thank you, and do so with deep gratitude. *Launching!* is the book it became because of you. I could not have done this without the assistance of a few very talented souls—Joyce Harvey-Morgan, Paige Kaye and Marlene Gast. Thank you so much. To my readers. Kim Howard, thank you for designing the most incredible book cover.

Deep gratitude to all of you who supported Vee, near and far-away, in those long nine months; to all the people who delivered meals made with love; to those of you who stopped me on the street to ask how my mother and I were doing. Your hugs and genuine heartfelt compassion soothed my aching heart. To Siouxze Essence for staying with Vee when I couldn't be there—bless you. To the healers who took care of Vee, thank you. To Linda Shoebridge, Dr. Maria Maricich, Jenifer Tyrer, Laurel Profit and Trinita Brunoehler – thank you so much for lovingly caring for my body. Your healing touch nourished every level of my being. To my worldwide sisterhood, may we continue our travels. Terry Choma, thank you for caring for Bailey. To Susan Randall, deep gratitude and love and thank you for loving my mother. Thank you, Holland, for purchasing a townhome so that I could be near my mother at the end of her life, and for allowing me to remain there until I completed the manuscript. There are no words to convey the enormity of this gift.

Every single person and event that comes into our lives does matter and is an opportunity for us to grow our souls, our relationship to ourselves, to each other, and to the world. We all have the choice to step into our lives more fully, to live with purpose and on purpose. For this reason, enormous gratitude to the two extraordinary people who supported me in finding my own way, and believed in me from the very beginning, my parents.

About the Author

Kate Riley is a certified death midwife, minister, educator, advocate, international story consultant, and author. She embarked on her life purpose in the field of death and dying after completing her hospice training in 1988. Kate had no idea at the time where it all would lead.

Kate lives in Idaho where she works as a home funeral guide and advocate/liaison for the dying and their families. Connecting with nature helps to renew her spirit, and she lives life passionately, spontaneously. Kate looks forward to traveling to Spain in the near future to visit her son, Sean, and his wife, Karolina.

kateriley.org

Printed in the United States
By Bookmasters